American Inside Out Evolution

Student's Book | Intermediate | B

SUE KAY
VAUGHAN JONES

macmillan education

Macmillan Education
Companies and representatives throughout the world
American Inside Out Evolution. Student's Book Intermediate B

Adapted by Peter Maggs and Catherine Smith / The Content Station team: Simon Campbell, George Wells and Catherine Gray
Macmillan is a registered trademark.
First edition published 2017

ISBN: 978-607-473-636-6

Based on New American Inside Out Student's Book Intermediate B

Editorial Manager: Patricia Muradas
Editorial Operations Coordinator: Veronica Teodorov Ferreira
Editor: Cintia Zaitune
Concept design: Martha Tadaieski
Page make-up: The Content Station
Illustrations: Karen Ahlschläger pp23, 39, 53, 60; Gustavo Gialuca pp14, 22, 30, 42, 47, 50.
Graphic Production: Kelly Gobbo
Photographic research: The Content Station
Cover concept and design: Jean Aranha
Cover photo: Vitaliy Pozdeev | Dreamstime

The authors and publishers would like to thank the following for permission to reproduce the photographic material:
Album / Touchstone Pictures p55 (r); **Dreamstime** / Photographerlondon pp8&9, Dreamstime / Ratz Attila p10(1), Dreamstime / Calvin Leake p10(2), Dreamstime / Tommaso79 p10(4), Dreamstime / Bigjiang p10(5), Dreamstime / Carrienelson1 p11, Dreamstime / Igor Kovalchuk p12(a), Dreamstime / Damed01 p12(b), Dreamstime / Toxawww p12(c), Dreamstime / Americanspirit p12(d), Dreamstime / Photographerlondon p12(e), Dreamstime / Stefan Dahl Langstrup p12(f), Dreamstime / Ilona Saibarakova p14 (News logo), Dreamstime / Petre Bucur p14 (woman), Dreamstime / Hongqi Zhang (aka Michael Zhang) p14 (man), Dreamstime / muratart p14 (TV), Dreamstime / Eric Overton p14 (house), Dreamstime / Prochasson Frederic p16, Dreamstime / Alekosa p17(a), Dreamstime / Juan Moyano p17(b), Dreamstime / Tomas Marek p17(c), Dreamstime / Paop p17(d), Dreamstime / Travnikovstudio p18(t), Dreamstime / Kobby Dagan p18(a), Dreamstime / Sven Hanscge p18(b), Dreamstime / Bvh2228 p18(c), Dreamstime / Manuelaudio p18(d), Dreamstime / Esviesa p19(t), Dreamstime / Serban Bogdan p19(b), Dreamstime / Wrangel p21, Dreamstime / Tom Wang p24, Dreamstime / Iuliia Lisitsyna p26(l), Dreamstime / Mikkolem p26(c), Antonio Guillem p26(r), Dreamstime / Sbukley p27(t), Dreamstime / Featureflash p27(b), Dreamstime / Nadino p28(a), Dreamstime / Opolja p28(b), Dreamstime / Dan Grytsku p28(c), Dreamstime / Volodymyr Melnyk p28(d), Dreamstime / Ruslan Huzau p28(e), Dreamstime / Nadino p28(f), Dreamstime / Roberto Caucino p28(t), Dreamstime / Yunuli123 p29(a), Dreamstime / Vbaleha p29(b), Dreamstime / Lekcej p29(c), Dreamstime / Mimagephotography p29(d), Dreamstime / Vadymvdroboto p37(t), Dreamstime / Jackbluee p37(b), Dreamstime / Oksun70 p38, Dreamstime / Weedezign p40, Dreamstime / Photoeuphoria p42, Dreamstime / Imagesolution p43, Dreamstime / Germanskydiver p46(l), Dreamstime / Julian Bound p48, Dreamstime / Photographerlondon p54(t), Dreamstime / Iryna Kalchenko p48 (br), Dreamstime / Sharplaninac p54(bl), Dreamstime / Sabphoto p55(a), Dreamstime / Anna Kraynova p55(b), Dreamstime / Makidotvn p55(c), Dreamstime / George Mayer p55(d), Dreamstime / Ampyang p56, Dreamstime / Viorel Dudau p63, Dreamstime / Subarashii21 pp65&66, Dreamstime / Robert Kneschke p71, Dreamstime / Antonio Guillem p73, Dreamstime / Ocskay Mark p75, Dreamstime / Doodkoalex p77, Dreamstime / Awlend p179, Dreamstime / Monkey Business Images p80; **Getty Images** / Kyodo News p46(r), Getty Images / Twentieth Century Fox Pictures / Sunset Boulevard p57(l), Getty Images / Frederick M Brown / Stringer p57(c); iStock / innovatedcaptures p58(all), iStock / alptraum / innovatedcaptures p64; Peter Emshwiller p50.

CANIEM No. 2275

Macmillan Publishers S.A. de C.V.
Insurgentes Sur 1886
Col. Florida, CP 01030
Álvaro Obregón
Ciudad de México
Tel: +52 (55) 5482 2200
elt@grupomacmillan.com

www.grupomacmillan.com www.macmillan.com.mx www.macmillanenglish.com

Printed in Brazil

This book was printed in December, 2017 by: Eskenazi Indústria Gráfica Ltda, Avenida Miguel Frias Vasconcelos, 1023 - Jaguaré - São Paulo - SP.

Contents

Walkthrough

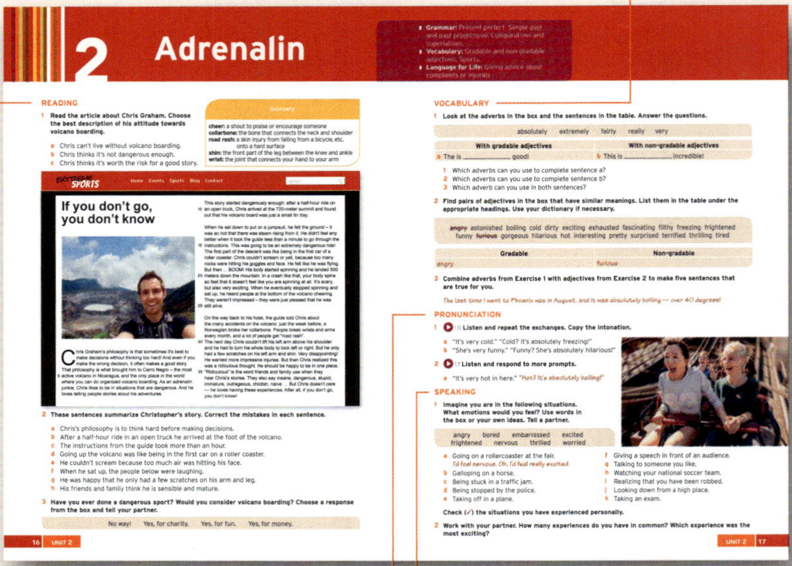

READING

Contemporary reading texts have been adapted and graded to suit each level. They have been selected not only for their language content but also for their interest and appropriacy. The texts are supported by recordings.

VOCABULARY

- Vocabulary is presented in a meaningful context and is related to the topics in the unit.
- Clear pictures help acquisition.
- There are practice activities to expand your knowledge of particular lexical sets and give you opportunities to use the new vocabulary in social exchanges.
- You will also listen to the words and repeat them before manipulating them in real social contexts.

PRONUNCIATION

Pronunciation work on particular areas of sound, stress, and intonation is integrated into every unit.

SPEAKING

You will have plenty of opportunities to speak throughout the unit using language learned.

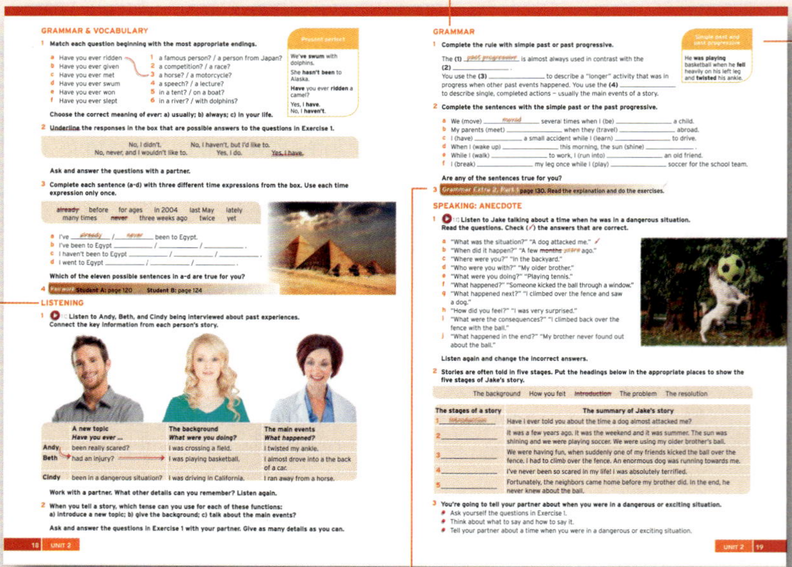

GRAMMAR

- Here you will explore new grammatical structures that have been contextualized in the reading / listening sections. You will focus on the way language works.
- A brief summary of the grammar point is provided in the box.
- Language is explored in realistic and meaningful practice exercises.
- You will use target language in controlled and personalized practice.

LISTENING

The listening activities include texts specially written for language learning – dialogues, conversations and monologues. They were carefully designed to develop real-life listening skills.

The Grammar Extra pages at the back of the Student's Book extend explanations and provide further practice.

LANGUAGE FOR LIFE

The Language for Life section gives you a portable toolkit of functional language. Here, you notice how language is more than just form. You will see language in fun, engaging social situations.

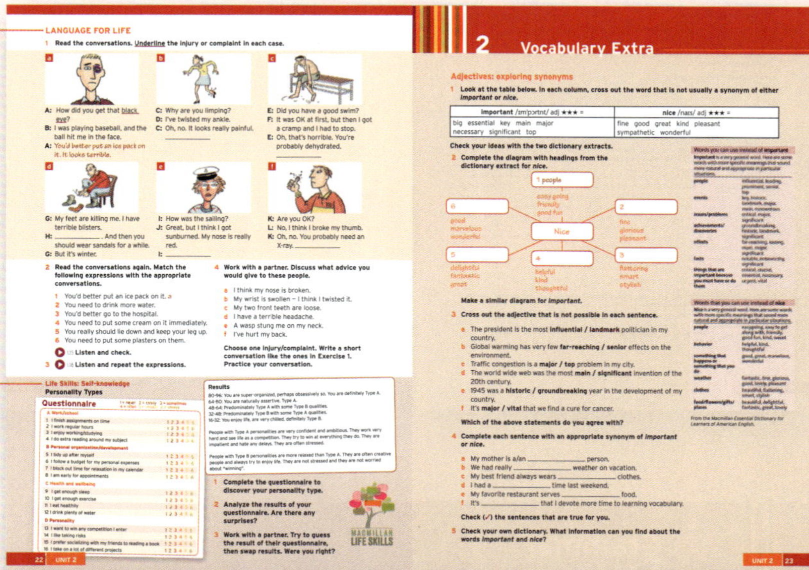

VOCABULARY EXTRA

The Vocabulary Extra pages at the end of every unit recycle the key vocabulary items taught in the unit. This provides an activated wordlist and a useful bank of vocabulary.

LIFE SKILLS

Developing life skills alongside language skills is an essential requirement to meet the demands of the contemporary world.

American Inside Out Evolution has a Life Skills section in every unit. Life Skills present activities in order for you to reflect on and discuss the skills you need for social and work situations in today's world.

REVIEW

There are Review units in the Student's Book. They review the new structures and vocabulary taught in the previous teaching units.

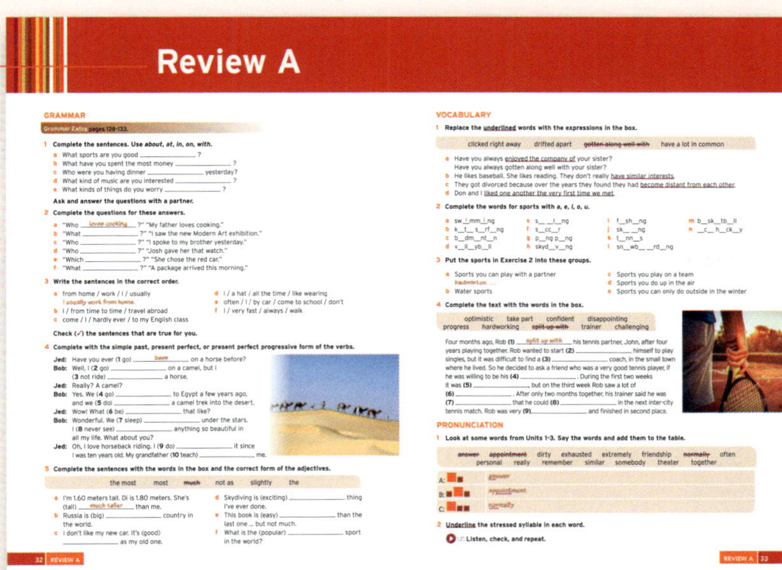

There is one Pairwork activity for every unit, which offers further speaking practice.

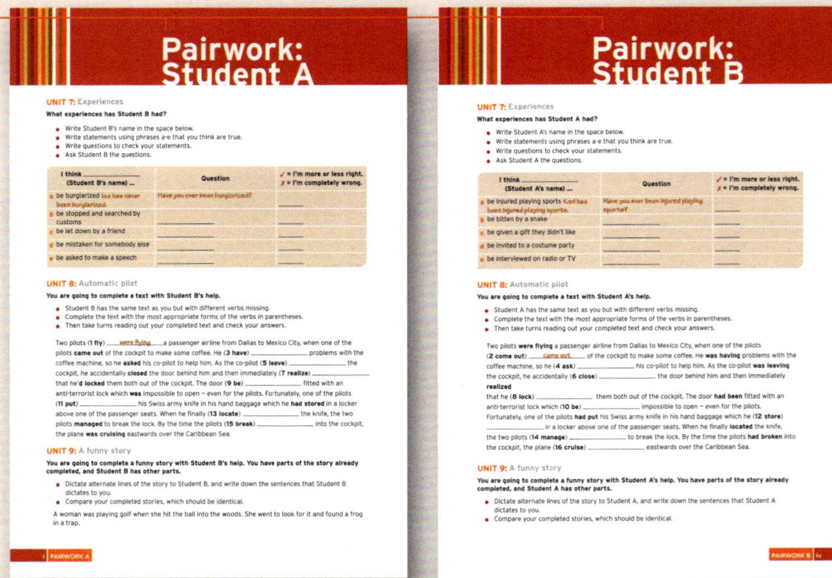
Pairwork: Student A

Pairwork: Student B

UNIT 7: Experiences

UNIT 8: Automatic pilot

UNIT 9: A funny story

GRAMMAR EXTRA

The Grammar Extra pages at the back of the Student's Book provide a summary of the new grammatical structures, as well as extra practice.

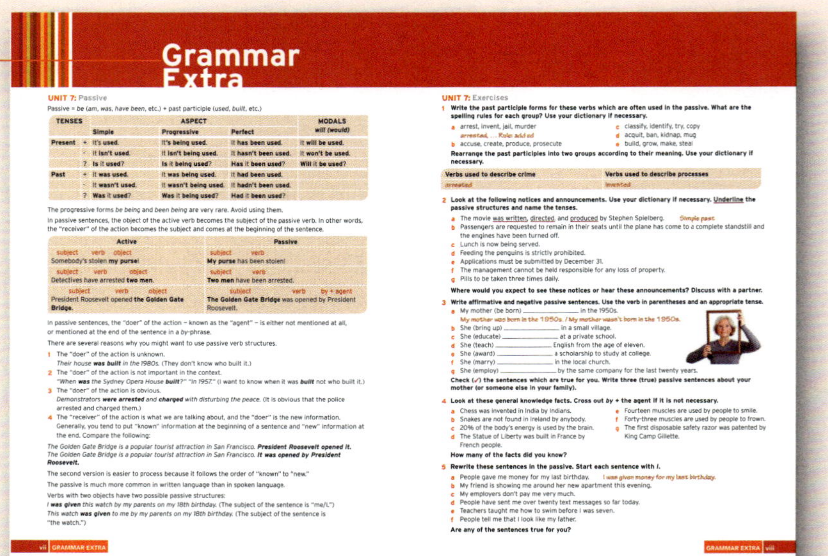
Grammar Extra

UNIT 7: Passive

UNIT 7: Exercises

The Workbook provides a review of all the main points in the Student's Book, plus extra listening practice, pronunciation work, and a writing program.

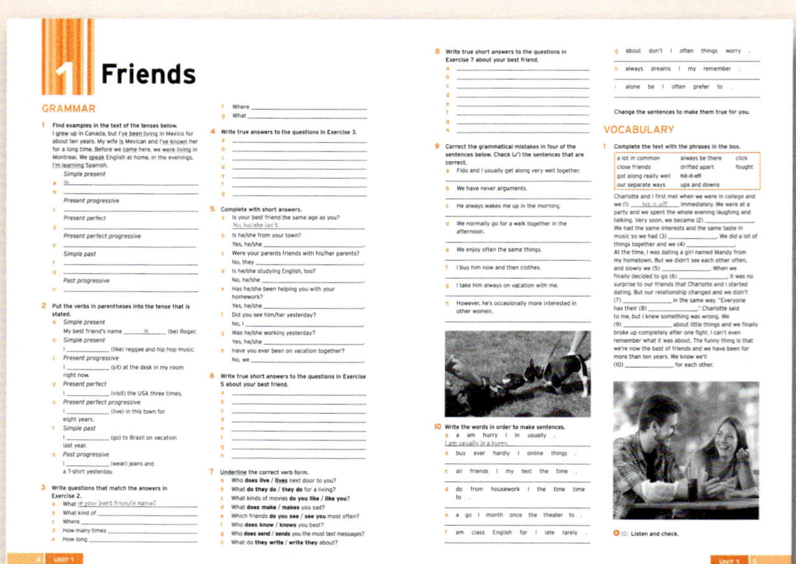
1 Friends

GRAMMAR

VOCABULARY

Student's Components

Student's Book with access code to Digital Student's Book

Workbook with access code to Digital Workbook

7 News

LISTENING

1 **Look at the picture and discuss the questions with a partner.**

a Who are the most photographed celebrities in your country?
b Which celebrities are in the news right now and why?
c How do you think celebrities feel about being photographed by the paparazzi?

2 **You are going to listen to an interview with Jack, an experienced paparazzo. What do you think his views are about the following? Underline *OK* or *not OK*.**

a **It's OK / not OK** when paparazzi take pictures of celebrities' glamorous lifestyles.
b **It's OK / not OK** when paparazzi take unflattering pictures of celebrities.
c **It's OK / not OK** when paparazzi take pictures of celebrities doing ordinary things.
d **It's OK / not OK** when paparazzi take pictures of celebrities' children.
e **It's OK / not OK** when paparazzi follow celebrities everywhere.
f **It's OK / not OK** when celebrities refuse to cooperate with the paparazzi.
g **It's OK / not OK** when celebrities complain about the paparazzi.

2.02 **Listen and check your ideas.**

Do you agree with Jack? Discuss your own views with a partner.

- **Grammar:** Verb patterns. Passive structures.
- **Vocabulary:** Adjectives. Crime. Headline language.
- **Language for Life:** Personal news

GRAMMAR

Verb patterns

I **can't stand waiting** around.
She **promised to come**.
We explained that it was difficult.
He **asked me to wait.**
They **told us that** they need time.

1 **Complete the following sentences about photographing celebrities. Use the verbs in the box.**

agrees asked enjoy explained tell

a People ____________ seeing pictures of celebrities doing ordinary things.
b Kate Moss ____________ us not to take photos of her daughter.
c We've ____________ that we don't want to upset her.
d Nicole Kidman always ____________ to smile for the camera.
e Celebrities ____________ us that we're invading their privacy.

2 **Use the verbs from Exercise 1 to complete the table of verb patterns.**

Verb + *ing*-form	Verb + *to*-infinitive	Verb + *that*	Verb + sb + (*not*) *to*-infinitive	Verb sb + *that*
• can't stand doing sth	• need to do sth	• realize that ...	• tell sb to do sth	• warn sb that ...
• don't mind doing sth	• promise to do sth	• say that ...	• warn sb not to do sth	• **(5)** ________ sb that ...
• **(1)** ________ doing sth	• try to do sth	• suggest that ...	• **(4)** ________ sb to do sth	
	• want to do sth	• think that ...		
	• **(2)** ________ to do sth	• **(3)** ________ that ...		

3 **In these statements two verbs are possible, and one is not. Cross out the verb that is not possible.**

a I **asked / told / ~~said~~** him to stop, but he pushed the camera in my face and continued taking pictures.
b I just **try / want / enjoy** to lead a normal life, but these people are making it impossible.
c When a celebrity gets aggressive, I **tell / explain / say** that I'm just doing my job.
d I **told / warned / suggested** him to stop taking photos of my daughter or I'd sue him.
e If they don't enjoy the attention, I **think / suggest / tell** that they should change jobs.
f They're hypocritical. On the one hand they **need / agree / don't mind** to have their pictures in the press, and on the other hand they **warn / tell / explain** us that we're invading their privacy.

Who do you think made each statement: a paparazzo or a celebrity? Compare your ideas with a partner.

VOCABULARY

1 **Complete the sentences with these adjectives from the interview in the Listening section.**

desperate hypocritical insensitive ~~obsessed~~ photogenic unflattering

a There is a lot of gossip about celebrities. Some people are *obsessed* with them!
b Some magazines print ____________ pictures of celebrities.
c I think it's ____________ to take pictures of celebrities when they are upset or sick. It's just not right.
d Some people say they're not interested in celebrities, but then read about them in magazines. I think they're ____________ .
e I hate pictures of myself because I always look terrible. I'm not very ____________ .
f Many fans are ____________ to see celebrities when they are showing up at a gala or festival.

2 **Are any of the views in Exercise 1 true for you? Discuss with a partner.**

READING & VOCABULARY

1 Match the news stories (1-5) with the headlines (a-e). Compare with a partner.

News in brief

HOME NEWS CONTACT

1
Pennsylvania police posted a mug shot of a burglar online yesterday, asking for information from the public. The man was a **fugitive** as he had escaped from prison last month. They were surprised when the criminal himself posted the photo on his own social media account. He added the comment, "Lol, I love it!" He was arrested 45 minutes later when he responded to a message inviting him for an interview. It was the police posing as journalists!

2
Twenty-eight-year-old James Allen was in court after the attempted robbery of a convenience store. He was **foiled** by the door! Holding a plastic gun and wearing a thick mask, he couldn't get the electric doors open. He then removed his mask in full view of the security camera before running away. A store employee recognized Allen when he came back to the store the next day. He will be sentenced next month.

3
Polish author Krystian Bala committed a **murder** and almost escaped punishment ... until he wrote a book that gave away clues! His novel *Amok* became a bestseller in Poland, but the police noticed that the details of a murder in the book were similar to a case they were investigating. The police discovered that the **victim** had been romantically involved with Bala's ex-wife. Bala was convicted and sentenced to 25 years in prison.

4
A San Francisco thief pedaled his bike up to a woman on the sidewalk, grabbed a phone out of her hands, and rode away. Unknown to him, the woman was in the middle of demonstrating the phone's new tracking device – which worked! The thief was **captured** just minutes later.

5
In El Paso, Texas, a man entered a church and got away with the safe. But safes are heavy, and he only got a few yards before dropping it on a neighbor's lawn. He tried to open it right there, and that's when he was met by the home's occupant – **a police officer**!

a SAFE AND SECURE
b SOCIAL MEDIA STUPIDITY
c UNMASKED
d A NOVEL CRIME
e TRACK IT DOWN

Which stories do you like best?

2 Complete the sentences using highlighted words from the stories in Exercise 1.

a A ___police officer___ is a person who fights crime and tries to catch criminals.
b A ________________ is someone who has been attacked or robbed.
c A ________________ is a crime involving the killing of a person.
d A ________________ is someone who has escaped from jail and is hiding from the police.
e A criminal is ________________ when they are prevented from carrying out a crime.
f When a criminal is ________________ they are taken prisoner.

3 Use these words from the stories in Exercise 1 to complete three more stories.

mug shot burglar arrested robbery convicted sentenced

NICE JUDGE
(1) ________________ Frank Gort broke down in court and cried when he was **(2)** ________________ to seven years in jail, claiming it was his unlucky number. An understanding judge in San Antonio, Texas gave him eight years instead.

LIKELY CRIMINAL
Jon Reardon, wanted for theft, loved his **(3)** ________________ on the Cascade Country Crimestoppers social media page so much, that he "liked" it. He was **(4)** ________________ a few weeks later.

SOCIAL MEDIA PROFILE
A couple, arrested this week for the **(5)** ________________ of an Ohio bank, posted photos on social media posing with the cash in the days after the crime. Known criminal John Morgan, a **(6)** ________________ robber, and his wife, Julie, also got tattoos celebrating their success.

PRONUNCIATION

1 ▶ 2.03 **Listen and repeat the past participle endings for regular verbs commonly used in the passive.**

ed = /t/	ed = /d/	ed = /ɪd/
asked based	believed called	arrested decided

ed **is pronounced as an extra syllable only after the sounds /t/ or /d/. True or false?**

2 **Practice saying the past participle for the verbs in the box. Add them to the correct column in the table in Exercise 1.**

check describe escape expect force involve name need report stop treat use

▶ 2.04 **Listen, check, and repeat.**

GRAMMAR

1 **Rewrite the following in the passive to recreate sentences from the news stories on page 66. Make the underlined words or phrases the subject of the passive verb.**

a Someone stole a safe. *A safe was stolen.*
b Someone captured the thief. *The thief ...*
c Someone arrested the man. *The man ...*
d Someone grabbed it. *It ...*

How is the passive formed? Find other examples of passive structures in the same news stories on page 66.

Passive

be + past participle

It **had been done**.
It **was done**.
It **was being done**.
It **has been done**.
It **is done**.
It **is being done**.
It **is going to be done**.
It **will be done**.

2 **Look at your sentences (a–d) above. Check (✓) the following explanations if you think they are correct.**

a In sentences *a*, *b*, *c*, and *d* the object of the active verb has become the subject of the passive verb.
b In sentences *a*, *b*, and *c* the "doer" of the action (= the agent) is either unknown, unimportant, or obvious.
c In sentence *d* the "doer" of the action (= the agent) is mentioned after the verb using *by*.

3 **Rewrite these newspaper extracts in the passive to make them sound more natural. Don't mention the agent.**

a The Oscar committee has announced the Oscar nominations.
The Oscar nominations have been announced.
b Doctors are treating the troubled movie star for "exhaustion" at Meadows Rehabilitation Center in Arizona.
c The record company has released the singer's long-awaited album to rave reviews.
d Kidnappers released the hostages last night and they are on their way home to their relieved families.
e The central bank will reduce interest rates by 1% before the end of the year according to most financial observers.
f People have accused the fashion industry of encouraging young girls to go on starvation diets.

Would you want to read more about any of the stories above?
What kinds of topics do you like reading about in the newspaper?

4 **Pairwork Student A:** page i **Student B:** page iv

5 **Grammar Extra 7** page vii. Read the explanation and do the exercises.

READING & LISTENING

1 Match each picture (a-f) with an appropriate newspaper headline (1-6).

1 ULTIMATE COSMIC COINCIDENCE
2 HIT AND RUN JOGGER ARRESTED
3 WILDFIRES RAGE IN SOUTHERN FRANCE
4 DELEGATES WALKOUT
5 PRESIDENT QUITS AFTER CORRUPTION PROBE
6 TATTOO STUDENT BARRED

What do you think each news item is about? Which story would you read first?

2 Find an underlined headline word in Exercise 1 that has the same meaning as the phrases below.

a unplanned departure *walkout*
b leaves his job
c are spreading out of control
d left the scene of an accident
e things happened at the same time
f the biggest and best
g has been excluded
h investigation

Are there any similar stories in the news today?

3 2.05 **Listen and match the radio news items (a-f) with the headlines (1-6) in Exercise 1.**

4 Work with a partner and complete the task.

- Write a news story based on one of the following three headlines (a-c).
- Invent any extra information you need.
- Broadcast your news to the rest of the class.

a FANS BARRED FROM SOCCER WORLD CUP FINAL
b CHIEF FIRE OFFICER QUITS AFTER FIRES RAGE AT BEACH RESORT
c HIT AND RUN DRIVER CAUGHT AFTER POLICE PROBE

READING & WRITING

1 Complete the email from Pia to her friend Ian. Use the words in the box.

Actually	Anyway	Apart	apparently	doing	forward
Good	~~great~~	happy	heard	let	news
sorry	touch				

mail.com

Compose
Inbox
Drafts
Sent
Spam
Trash

To: ian@mail.com
Cc:
Subject:
From: pia@mail.com

Hi Ian,
Thanks for your email. It was **(1)** ___great___ to hear from you. I'm **(2)** ________ I haven't replied sooner, but work's been really stressful. More about that in a minute. But first, I was really **(3)** ________ to hear about your promotion. You deserve it – you've worked so hard. **(4)** ________ job! I wish you were still living in Berlin, so we could go out and celebrate. Anyway, back to my stressful job! **(5)** ________, it's much better now that there has been some restructuring within the company.
The good **(6)** ________ is that we've got a new boss, and he's quite dynamic. He's already made a few changes, and the best thing is that he wants me to travel more, so I'll be able to see all my friends back home more often.
Talking of friends, have you **(7)** ________ about Anna and Giorgio? They've split up! I have no idea why, but **(8)** ________, Giorgio's gone back to Italy and Anna's refusing to talk to anybody about it. Please **(9)** ________ me know if you hear any more about it.
(10) ________ from that, everything's fine here in Berlin. It's getting pretty hot, and I'm looking **(11)** ________ to going on vacation in August. What are your vacation plans?
(12) ________, I'd better get back to work now, but be in **(13)** ________ soon and tell me how you're **(14)** ________.

Lots of love,
Pia

2 Read the email again and answer the questions.

a Who lives in Berlin?
b Who used to live in Berlin?
c Who got promoted at work?
d Who's got a new boss?
e Who's split up?
f Who's gone back to Italy?

3 Work with a partner. Use the sentence beginnings below to invent a reply from Ian to Pia's email.

mail.com

Compose
Inbox
Drafts
Sent
Spam
Trash

To: pia@mail.com
Cc:
Subject:
From: ian@mail.com

Dear Pia,

It was great …
I'm sorry …
I was so happy …
By the way, Giorgio called me. Apparently …
Apart from that, I'm looking forward to my vacation. I'm going …
Anyway, …

Lots of love,

P.S. Guess what! …

Compare your email with other people in the class. Choose the email with the best ideas.

LANGUAGE FOR LIFE

1 **Match the two pictures to two of the conversations (a-h).**

1

2

a **A:** How's Leanne?
B: Actually, we've split up.
A: Oh, I'm sorry to hear that. / How exciting!
B: It's OK. Um, this is Cassandra.

b **C:** Hello. You're looking really happy with yourself.
D: I am! I just passed my driving test!
C: Oh, no. That's terrible! / Good job! Was it your first time?
D: No, my sixth.

c **E:** Guess what! I've won a vacation to Florida.
F: I'm sorry to hear that. / Lucky you! Is it a vacation for two?
E: Yes, I'm taking my mom.
F: Oh.

d **G:** You don't look very happy.
H: No, I just got my exam scores. I failed them all.
G: Good job! / Oh, no, that's terrible! What happened?
H: I didn't do any work.

e **I:** Do you like this bunch of flowers? They are for my wife.
J: They are lovely! What are you celebrating?
I: We've just had a baby.
J: Oh, congratulations! / How annoying!

f **K:** You don't usually take the bus!
L: No – my car's broken down again.
K: How annoying! / Good job!
L: I know. But it is twenty-five years old.

g **M:** What did you do last night?
N: I watched a documentary about snow leopards.
M: Oh, that sounds interesting. / Oh, I'm sorry to hear that.
N: Yes ... unfortunately, I fell asleep halfway through.

h **O:** What are you doing today?
P: I'm taking my first sailing class.
O: How exciting! / Oh, no, that's terrible! Are you nervous?
P: I am actually. I can't swim.

2 **Work with a partner. Read the conversations (a-h) which show people responding to good and bad news. In each case, underline the appropriate response.**

2.06 **Listen and check.**

3 **Classify the useful phrases that you heard in Exercise 2 in the table below.**

Positive responses	Negative responses
	Oh, I'm sorry to hear that.

2.07 **Listen, check, and repeat.**

4 2.08 **Listen to some more pieces of good and bad news and respond appropriately.**

Life Skills: Accessing and Analyzing Information

A Hurricane

1 **Discuss with a partner where you go for the news.**

a

9 a.m. August 24

b

10 a.m. August 24

c

At least 2 die in Hurricane Lucy

Hurricane Lucy hit the US early on Thursday morning. All the roads coming from the Texas coast were full of cars. The mayor of Rockport, Texas, told residents who decided to stay to write their social security number on their arm. This would help rescue services identify them.

Sunday August 27

d

2 a.m. August 24

Which of the above media published the story first? Which do you think is the most accurate? Why?

7 Vocabulary Extra

Verb patterns

1 Complete the common verb patterns (a-j) with *ask*, *explain*, *say*, or *tell*.

a ___*explain*___ / **say** + (that)

b **explain** / ________ / **say** how/ what, etc.

c ________ / **say** sth to sb

d ________ sth on / about

e ________ sb + (that)

f ________ / **tell** sb why/ how, etc.

g ________ / **ask** sb sth

h ________ / **tell** sb about sth

i ________ sb for sth

j ________ / **tell** sb to do sth

Check your answers in the dictionary extracts. Which verbs almost always have a person (sb) as a direct object?

2 Say or tell? Underline the correct verbs in these sentences.

a She **said / told** that she liked dancing.

b Didn't he **say / tell** you that I wanted to see you?

c I want to **say / tell** something about this subject.

d Just **say / tell** me what she **said / told**.

e "**Say / Tell** me about your day," she **said / told**.

f I haven't been **said / told** anything about it.

Check your answers in the dictionary extracts.

3 Complete the joke with the correct form of either *say* or *tell*.

Sherlock Holmes and Dr. Watson went on a camping trip. As they lay down for the night, Holmes **(1)** ___*said:*___ "Watson, look up into the sky and **(2)** ________ me what you see."
Watson **(3)** ________ : "I see millions and millions of stars."
Holmes: "And what does that **(4)** ________ you?" Watson: "Astronomically, it **(5)** ________ me that there are millions of galaxies and potentially billions of planets. In relative terms, it **(6)** ________ me that we are small and insignificant. Meteorologically, it **(7)** ________ me that we will have a beautiful day tomorrow. What does it **(8)** ________ you?"
Holmes: "Somebody stole our tent."

4 Complete the questions with the most appropriate verb: *asked*, *explained*, *said*, or *told*.

When was the last time you ...

a ___*told*___ your friends a joke?

b ________ no to chocolate?

c ________ somebody to "cheer up"?

d ________ what you do for a living?

e ________ somebody for a ride?

f ________ sorry to a friend?

g ________ a friend to help you?

h ________ the rules of a game to somebody?

i ________ that you needed to do some exercise?

j ________ somebody that you loved them?

Work with a partner. Ask and answer the questions.

5 Check your own dictionary. What example sentences does it include to illustrate the different verb patterns for *ask*, *explain*, *say*, and *tell*?

---

ask /æsk/ verb ★★★
1 [I/T] to speak to someone in order to get information from them: *I wondered who had given her the ring but was afraid to ask.* ♦ *The police wanted to* ***ask*** *us a few* ***questions.*** ♦ **ask (sb) why/how/whether etc.** *She asked me how I knew about it.* ♦ **ask (sb) about sth** *Did you ask about the money?*
2 [I/T] to speak to someone because you want them to give you something, or do something for you: *If you need any help, just ask.* ♦ *Can I ask you a favor?* ♦ **ask (sb) for sth** *The children were asking for drinks.* ♦ **ask sb to do sth** *He asked us to move over a little.* ♦ **ask to do sth** *I asked to see the manager.* ♦ **ask (sb) if/whether** *Ask if we can go backstage.*

ex•plain /ɪk'spleɪn/ verb ★★★
1 [T] to tell someone something in a way that helps them to understand it better: **explain sth to sb** *The doctor explained the risks to me before the operation.* ♦ **+how/when/what etc.** *I will try to explain how a car engine works.* ♦ **+(that)** *He explained that he would be moving to another city.*

say[1] /seɪ/ (3rd person singular **says** /sez/; past tense and past participle **said** /sed/) verb ★★★

1 express with words	4 show sth
2 have opinion	5 imagine sth
3 give information	+ PHRASES

1 [I/T] to express something using words: *"Nice to meet you," he said with a smile.* ♦ *"When's he coming back?" "He didn't say."* ♦ *The committee* ***said yes*** (=gave permission), *so we can go ahead.* ♦ *What a strange* ***thing to say,*** *Carrie thought.* ♦ *I then* ***said goodbye*** *and left.* ♦ *I already* ***said sorry for*** *hurting his feelings.* ♦ **+(that)** *She said that she liked dancing.* ♦ **+how/what/who etc.** *Did he say who called?* ♦ **say sth to sb** *Tell me what he said to you.* ♦ **say sth on/about** *I want to say something about this subject.*

tell /tel/ (past tense and past participle **told** /toʊld/) verb ★★★

1 sb gives information	6 see difference
2 sth gives information	7 have clear effect
3 talk about story	8 fail to keep secret
4 order/advise to do sth	+ PHRASES
5 know sth	+ PHRASAL VERBS

1 [T] to give information to someone: *If you see anything suspicious, tell the police.* ♦ **tell sb (that)** *Didn't he tell you that I wanted to see you?* ♦ **tell sb who/what/why/how etc.** *Just tell me what she said.* ♦ **tell sb sth** *He finally told me the reason he was so upset.* ♦ **tell sb (sth) about sth** *"Tell me about your day," she said.* → SAY
2 [T] if something such as a fact, event, or piece of equipment tells you something, it gives you or shows you some information: *The flashing light tells you when the battery needs recharging.* ♦ *What does this room tell you about the person who lived here?*
3 [T] if you tell a story or a joke, you give someone a spoken account of it: *Grandpa* ***tells*** *wonderful* ***stories*** *about the old days.* ♦ **tell sb sth** *I have to tell you this joke.*
4 [T] to order or strongly advise someone to do something: *I'm not asking you – I'm telling you!* ♦ **tell sb to do sth** *I told you to be here on time this morning.* ♦ **tell sb what/how/when etc.** *I told him what to do, but he wouldn't listen.*

From the *Macmillan Essential Dictionary for Learners of American English.*

8 Travel

READING

1 **Have you ever traveled for any of these reasons? Discuss with a partner.**

- to broaden your experience of the world
- to run away from a broken heart
- to learn a language (or something else)
- to take a break from your career
- to visit historical sites
- to get a suntan

2 **Read this travel review. When did the author's dad propose to his mom in Venice?**

Moonlit Venice

by Steph Mortimer

This trip lived up to all my expectations. I have wanted to go to Venice ever since I discovered that my dad proposed to my mom there. I had obviously heard a lot about the place, read lots of books, and looked at hundreds of photographs. But nothing prepares you for the reality of it. It is so beautiful. Around every corner, there is another lovely building or picturesque square. The architecture is stunning. I managed to find a very good hotel not far from the famous Rialto Bridge. It's on a small central square, but was very quiet at night. (This was a relief, as I'm a very light sleeper and wake at the slightest sound – even with earplugs in!) I spent my days walking all over the city, soaking up the beauty of it all. In the evenings, I ate really good Italian food. Many of the cafés and restaurants are very expensive, but you can find cheaper places if you are prepared to walk a bit. One night, I set out to find the little square where my dad went down on one knee 55 years ago. In the moonlight, it looked so pretty and romantic. I understood why my dad had chosen that place. Venice is so special. If you have never been there I urge you to go – seeing is believing! I will be going again as soon as I can.

3 **Are these statements true or false?**

a The author has wanted to go to Venice since her parents' wedding.
b She has done her homework on Venice.
c Her hotel was located in a very busy street.
d She couldn't sleep at night.
e She ate Italian food in the evenings.
f She found the restaurant where her dad proposed 55 years ago.

Is there a place that is special for your family? Would you like to go there?

Glossary

live up to sth (phrasal verb): to be as good as what was expected or promised

manage to do sth: to succeed in doing sth

soak up: (INFORMAL) to spend time experiencing, listening to, or feeling something enjoyable

urge someone to do sth: to advise strongly

SPEAKING

1 **Work with your partner. Make a list of different places you've traveled to.**

2 **Choose five places from your list and think about how to describe where they are. Use the expressions in the box.**

It's in the	north/southwest	of (Japan).
	southern/ northeastern part	of (Peru).

	on the coast	to the north of (Vigo).
It's	in the mountains	not far from (Jalapa).
	in (Pernambuco)	between (Recife) and (Olinda).

Tell your partner where, when, and why you traveled to these places.

- **Grammar:** Modals of deduction. Past perfect.
- **Vocabulary:** Location. Describing places. Fixed expressions.
- **Language for Life:** Asking for and giving directions

a

b

c

d

READING & VOCABULARY

1 Look at the photographs of popular places. Which one would you most like to visit and why? Read the description below. Which picture does it describe?

Visiting this place is a life-changing experience. If you are in this part of the world, you must include it in your itinerary. To get here is difficult, but ultimately rewarding. It involves four days of cold, pain, and exhaustion. But when the mist lifts to reveal the emerald peaks and terraced ruins of this ancient place, I promise you will forget all the hardship. The best time to visit is May through September. Although this is the busiest time, it is also the driest. Believe me, this is not a place you want to visit in the rainy season. You'll need to take strong walking boots and a torch with spare batteries. If you want to join an organized tour, you'll also need to make your reservation many months in advance, as it is a very popular destination.

2 Read the paragraph again. Are these sentences true or false?

a The writer thinks this is a good place to visit.
b Getting to the place is easy.
c May to September is the rainy season.
d The busiest time to arrive is also when there is the least rain.
e You must book your place on a tour a long time before you arrive.
f You'll need smart shoes.

3 Work with a partner. Complete the two descriptions below using words and expressions in the box.

contests spectators era ~~attractions~~ damaged constructed Italy island sailing chased ship sea blue

The Colosseum is one of the most famous and popular tourist **(1)** attractions in Rome, **(2)** ________. It was **(3)** ________ between AD 72 and 80, and is still the largest amphitheater ever built. It could hold between 50,000 and 80,000 **(4)** ________, who came to watch the popular gladiator **(5)** ________ and other public events. Since the early medieval **(6)** ________, the Colosseum has stopped being an entertainment venue. It has been **(7)** ________ by earthquakes and stone robbers, but it remains an icon of ancient Rome and its emperors.

This beautiful place is on the northwest coast of the Greek island of Zakynthos. It was named Shipwreck Beach after a container **(8)** ________ ended up on the beach here on October 2, 1980. The M V Panagiotis was **(9)** ________ from Turkey to Italy with, it is believed, illegal goods on board. It was being **(10)** ________ by the Greek navy when stormy weather forced it into the small cove. The crew abandoned ship and ran off. The remains of the ship still lie on the beach. The beach can only be reached from the **(11)** ________ and is loved for its white sand and clear **(12)** ________ water. There are regular boat tours from other parts of the **(13)** ________.

4 Work with a partner. Talk about places in your city or country ...

a that are unspoiled.
b where there are wonderful beaches.
c where the views are spectacular.
d where young people go to hang out and be seen.
e where you can hardly move because it's so crowded on the weekend.
f that are popular with foreign tourists.

LISTENING

1 **Look at pictures (a-d) taken on Conrad's around-the-world trip. Where do you think they were taken?**

a

b

c

d

2.09 **Listen to Amy and Joe discussing the pictures on Conrad's blog and check your ideas. Number the pictures in the order they mention them.**

2 **Match the words in the box with the pictures (a-d) in Exercise 1.**

river	Buddhist temples	a built-up skyline	forests
horseman	high-rise buildings	snow-capped mountains	waterfalls

Are there any places in your country where you can see these things? Tell a partner.

GRAMMAR

Modals of deduction

The lights aren't on:

Sam **must** be out. (= certain)

He **can't** be in. (= certain)

He **might**/**may**/**could** be away for the weekend or on vacation or ... (= possible)

1 **Complete these explanations of the modal structures from the discussion on page 74. Use *must* or *can't*.**

a I think it's certain = "It __________ be Singapore ... I know he stopped off there."

b I think it's possible = "It might/ may/ could be Vietnam."

c I think it's impossible = "It __________ be India, because he hasn't been there yet."

2 **Look at the information in the table and try and name the countries (a-f) from the list in the box. Discuss your ideas with a partner.**

Angola Argentina Spain Uruguay Brazil Cuba Mexico Mozambique Peru Portugal

Country	Population (country)	Population (biggest city)	Official language	Highest mountain	Main exports
a __________	Over 45 million	About 3 million	Spanish	3,718 m	chemicals, fruit, cars
b __________	Over 10 million	Over half a million	Portuguese	2,351 m	chemicals, cork, leather
c __________	Over 208 million	Over 12 million	Portuguese	3,014 m	animal feed, chemicals, coffee
d __________	Nearly 130 million	Nearly 9 million	Spanish	5,700 m	chemicals, coffee, cotton
e __________	Over 43 million	Nearly 3 million	Spanish	6,962 m	animal oils, meat
f __________	Over 25 million	Nearly 3 million	Portuguese	2,619 m	oil, diamonds

Write sentences with *must be*, *might be*, or *can't* be to show how you decided.

Country "c" must be Brazil, because it's the country with the biggest population and they speak Portuguese there.

Have you ever been to any of these countries? Tell your partner.

3 **Grammar Extra 8, Part 1 page ix. Read the explanation and do the exercises.**

PRONUNCIATION

1 2.10 **Listen and repeat the words in the box. Mark the main stress.**

the Amazon the Andes Antarctica Asia the Atlantic the Danube Europe the Himalayas the Indian Ocean the Nile the Pacific the Pyrenees

2 **List the words in the correct column according to size (from largest to smallest).**

	Continents	Mountain ranges	Oceans	Rivers
+ ↓ -	*Asia*			

2.11 **Listen, check, and repeat.**

READING & LISTENING

1 Read the text conversation between two friends. What was Nick's motivation for the trip?

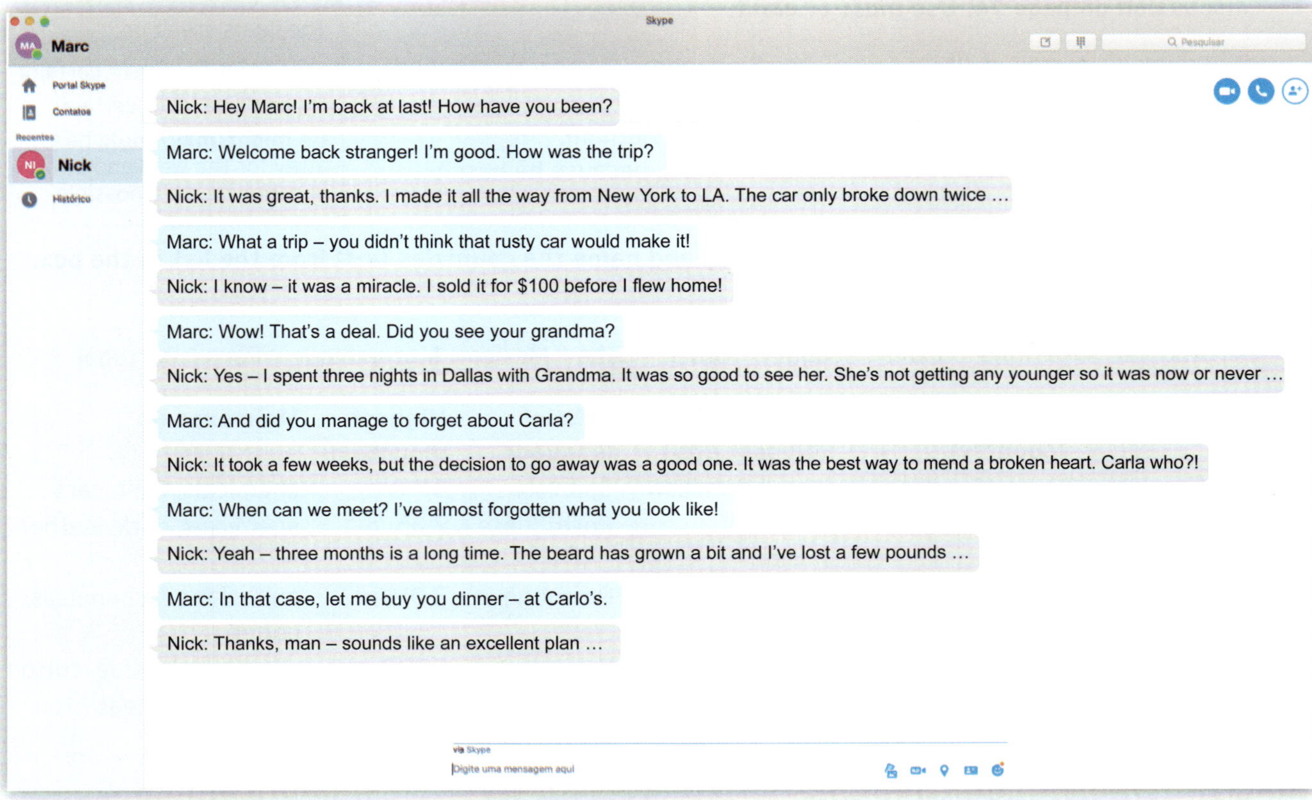

2 Work with a partner. Discuss these questions.

- **a** How long has Nick been away?
- **b** How much did Nick sell his car for?
- **c** How many times did Nick's car break down?
- **d** What did Marc offer to buy Nick?
- **e** Who do you think Carla is?

3 ▶ 2.12 **Listen to the conversation between Nick and Marc. What do you think Marc said next?**

VOCABULARY

1 Look at this expression from the conversation above. What does it mean?

"… so it was now or never."

- **a** either now or in the future
- **b** only now and not in the future

2 Work with a partner. Use words from the box to complete some more fixed expressions.

all	tidy	come	give	peace	Sooner	~~take~~

- **a** I don't particularly like watching TV. I can ____take____ **it or leave it**.
- **b** When I go on vacation, all I want is some ________________ **and quiet**.
- **c** I vacuum my car regularly because I like it to be **neat and** ________________.
- **d** It's 200 kilometers to the coast from here, ________________ **or take** a few kilometers.
- **e** My computer is getting old. ________________ **or later**, I'll have to buy a new one.
- **f** I don't eat chocolate for weeks. Then I'll eat three bars in one day! It's ________________ **or nothing** with me.
- **g** My teenagers treat our house like a hotel. They just ________________ **and go** as they please.

Are any of the sentences true for you?

GRAMMAR

1 **This is Nick's route across the USA. Refer to the conversation on page 76 and answer these questions.**

a Where did Nick begin his journey?
b Where did Nick stop to visit his grandma?
c Where did Nick sell his car?

2 **Look at these statements about Nick's trip and choose the correct verb from the box.**

stopped bought texted ~~split~~ broke down flew drove

a Nick had ___split___ with his girlfriend before he went away.
b Before the trip, Nick had ________ an old car.
c The car only ________ ________ twice.
d Nick ________ all the way from New York to Los Angeles.
e In Dallas, Nick ________ to visit his grandmother.
f Nick ________ home from Los Angeles to New York.
g When Nick got home, he ________ his friend, Marc.

Past perfect

had + past participle

We were too late: the train **had** already **left**.

I knew I **hadn't been** there before.

Why are the events which took place before his trip described in the past perfect?

3 **Work with a partner. Complete each of these sentences with a verb in the past perfect to make up a story about Michael's journey to Venezuela.**

a Michael was looking forward to his business trip to Venezuela because ...
b He was late leaving the house because ...
c The traffic was very slow from his house to the airport because ...
d At the check-in, he had to accept a seat at the back of the plane because ...
e The departure was delayed because ...
f As the plane was taking off, he suddenly remembered that ...

Compare your ideas with other people in the class.

4 **Pairwork Student A:** page i. **Student B:** page iv.

5 **Grammar Extra 8, Part 2** page ix. Read the explanation and do the exercises.

SPEAKING: ANECDOTE

1 2.13 **Listen to Suzi talking about a trip she has been on. Cross out the wrong information in each of her answers.**

a Where did the trip start? **The Dead Sea.**
b Where did the trip finish? **St. Christopher's Monastery.**
c What was the reason for the trip? **I couldn't go diving.**
d What form of transportation did you use? **A big van.**
e What was the weather like? **Hot and windy.**
f Who did you go with? **Seven tourists, a guide, and a driver.**
g How long did it take you? **Three hours.**
h What did you do during the trip? **I looked out of the window at the ocean.**
i Did you stop en route? What for? **Yes, to take pictures and buy food.**
j Would you go on the same trip again? Why? **Yes, but in my own car.**

Correct the information. Listen again and check.

2 **You are going to tell your partner about a trip you have been on.**

- Ask yourself the questions in Exercise 1.
- Think about what to say and how to say it.
- Tell your partner about your trip.

LANGUAGE FOR LIFE

1 2.14 **Read and listen to a conversation between a couple in a car. Answer the questions.**

a Where do they want to go?
b Which number road are they looking for?
c How many times do they pass the movie theater?

Angie: Rick, do you know where we are?
Rick: Yes, of course. Why?
Angie: Because we've passed the same movie theater twice.
Rick: Oh, no.
Angie: You'd better stop and ask somebody.
Rick: OK. ... Excuse me, I'm trying to get to Sacramento. Do you know how we can get onto Route 80 from here?
Man 1: Yes, first you need to turn around and then take the first left. Go to the end of the road and you'll come to a stop sign. Take a right and you'll see Route 80.
Rick: Great, thanks. ... Did he say left or right?
Angie: I can't remember. Look, stop and ask that woman.
Rick: Excuse me, we're looking for the road to Sacramento. Could you tell me which way we need to go?
Woman: Sacramento? Go straight down here until you come to a gas station. Then turn left and follow the signs.
Rick: OK, thanks. ... I haven't seen the gas station yet.
Angie: No, neither have I, but here's that movie theater again.
Rick: Oh, no. ... Excuse me, we're lost. Do you have any idea where Route 80 is?
Man 2: Er, no, sorry.

2 **Read the conversation again and complete the useful phrases.**

Saying what you're looking for
a Excuse me, I'm trying *to get to* Sacramento.
b Excuse me, we're looking ________ Sacramento.

Asking for directions
c Do you know how ________ Route 80?
d Could you tell me which ________ ?
e Do you have any idea where ________ ?

Giving directions
f You need to turn ________ and then ________ left.
g Go to the end of the road and you'll ________ .
h Go straight down here until ________ .
i Turn left and follow ________ .

2.15 **Listen, check, and repeat.**

3 **Work with a partner. Rewrite the following questions in less direct language. Refer to the expressions (c-e) in Exercise 2 and start your questions with *Do you know ...? Could you tell me ...?* or *Do you have any idea ...?***

a Where's the nearest bank?
Excuse me. Do you know where the nearest bank is?
b How can I get to the airport from here?
c I'm looking for the bus station. Which way do I need to go?
d How can I get downtown from here?
e Where can I get a taxi?
f How can I get to the shopping mall from here?

Ask each other the questions and give appropriate directions from where you are now.

Life Skills: Problem-solving

A Flight Mystery

1 2.16 **Listen to the story of Tim, the lost traveler. Where was he spotted last?**

2 **Look at these statements. Rank them in order, from most to least likely. Discuss with your partner.**

He must still be in the United States. ☐
He might be in the UK under a different passport. ☐
He took the wrong flight and hasn't been able to get back to the UK. ☐
He might be in trouble with the police. ☐
He changed his mind and went on vacation instead. ☐
Something bad has happened to Tim. ☐

3 **Where do you think Tim is? Work in small groups and decide on an explanation for his disappearance. Use modals of deduction (*must, can't, might*, etc.) in your discussions.**

MACMILLAN LIFE SKILLS

8 Vocabulary Extra

Dictionary labels

1 **Match the dictionary labels with their definitions.**

a British	1 Not used in everyday speech or writing.
b American	2 Used in American English, but not in British English.
c formal	3 Used commonly in speech, but not in writing.
d informal	4 Used in British English, but not in American English.

2 **Use an appropriate label from Exercise 1 as a heading for the word lists (1-3).**

1	2	3
sweets	guy	alight
pavement	nerd	beverage
rubbish bin		refrain

Check your answers in the dictionary extracts.

3 **Work with a partner. Decide what each sign means and where you might see it. Use the dictionary extracts to help you.**

1

2

3

4

a Foot passengers please disembark via the steps at the front of the ferry
b All cyclists must dismount here
c The use of calculators is not permissible
d Do not alight from the train whilst it is still in motion

Write less formal versions of each notice.

1 *Please don't use your calculator.*

4 **Rewrite these sentences in American English.**

a Last year, I took my holiday in the autumn.
Last year, I went on vacation in the fall.
b We keep our rubbish bin on the pavement in front of our house.
c I never eat sweets or biscuits between meals.
d I get angry with lorry drivers who go too fast on the motorway.
e There's a postbox near the Underground station.

Are any of the sentences true for you?

5 **Check your own dictionary. What kinds of labels does it use?**

alight[2] /əˈlaɪt/ verb [I] *formal* to get off a train, bus, or other vehicle

autumn /ˈɔtəm/ noun [C/U] *British* fall

beverage /ˈbev(ə)rɪʤ/ noun [C] *formal* a drink

biscuit /ˈbɪskɪt/ noun [C] *British* cookie

disembark /ˌdɪsɪmˈbɑrk/ verb [I] *formal* to get off a ship or plane

dismount /dɪsˈmaʊnt/ verb [I] *formal* to get off a horse or a bike

guy /gaɪ/ noun [C] ★★ *informal* a man

highway /ˈhaɪˌweɪ/ noun [C] ★ a wide road that has been built for fast travel between towns and cities

holiday /ˈhɑlɪˌdeɪ/ noun [C/U] ★★★ *British* a vacation

lorry /ˈlɔri/ noun [C] *British* a truck

motorway /ˈmoʊtərˌweɪ/ noun [C] *British* a large highway

nerd /nɜrd/ noun [C] *informal* someone who is boring and not fashionable

pavement /ˈpeɪvmənt/ noun [C] *British* a sidewalk

permissible /pərˈmɪsəb(ə)l/ adj *formal* if something is permissible, you are allowed to do it

persons /ˈpɜrs(ə)nz/ noun [C] *formal* the plural of person is people, but in formal or official language the form persons is used

postbox /ˈpoʊstˌbɑks/ noun [C] *British* a mailbox

purchase[1] /ˈpɜrtʃəs/ verb [T] *formal* to buy something

refrain /rɪˈfreɪn/ verb [I] *formal* to stop yourself from doing something

rubbish bin /ˈrʌbɪʃ ˌbɪn/ noun [C] *British* trash can

sweets /swits/ noun [C] *British* candy

Underground, the /ˈʌndərˌgraʊnd/ noun [singular] *British* the subway

From the *Macmillan Essential Dictionary for Learners of American English*.

9 Opinions

SPEAKING & READING

1 **In pairs discuss:**

Why do people go on social media?

Do young people and adults go on different reasons?

2 **Complete the questionnaire. Then compare your answer with your partner.**

www.survey.com

Dashboard My Surveys Products Resources Plans & Pricing

One thousand Americans between the ages of 18 and 35 were interviewed for a survey about attitudes to social media. These are the questions they were asked.
Check the answers a), b), or c) for the answer which most applies to you.

WHAT DO YOU USE SOCIAL MEDIA FOR?

1 ... for politics?
a I like to share how I vote on social media.
b I prefer to keep my voting record private in case I offend my friends.
c I find it boring to read about people's political views on social media.

2 ... for food?
a I like to post successful recipes so that my friends can enjoy good food too.
b I read food blog posts and watch demo videos but rarely cook anything myself.
c I surf the net for good recipes when I am having friends round for a meal.

3 ... for travel?
a I think that the internet is the best tool for researching destinations and booking trips.
b I post blogs about my trips so that my friends and others can share my experiences.
c I don't like to reveal where I have been in case my secret spots get ruined by tourists.

4 ... for shopping?
a I mainly buy clothes on the net.
b I look at favourite brands on the net, select some pieces, then go to the mall to try them on.
c I mainly buy from stores.

5 ... for entertainment?
a I download or stream most of my videos and movies from the net.
b I use the net for catch-up TV.
c I rarely use the internet for entertainment.

6 ... for news?
a I get the news from social media rather than from the newscasts or newspapers.
b I look at Twitter first when a news item breaks.
c I rarely use social media for news.

- **Grammar:** Reported statements and questions
- **Vocabulary:** Books. Movies. Music. *ed/ing* adjectives.
- **Language for Life:** Giving your opinion

Glossary

Trend (n.): gradual change
Overrun (v.): occupy in large numbers in a way that it is umpleasant.
Purchase (n.): the action of buying something
Catch up on sth (phrasal verb): to do something that should have been done before
Newscasts (n.): a news program

READING

1 **Read about the findings which came out of the survey about social media.**
Complete the results with the most appropriate word from the box.

surfed political bookings ~~entertainment~~ newspapers downloaded stores quiet

No one wants to appear superficial when using social media. Nowadays it seems most people want to make a statement when they post on the internet. Many people turn to different online environments where they can tell their friends their opinions on a great variety of issues, such as politics, food, travel, shopping, **(1)** *entertainment*, news, etc. See below for current trends in internet use.

On politics: 63% of people said that they liked to express how they voted on social media whereas 30% *didn't like* to risk causing offence to friends so preferred to keep their political opinions private. A minority, 7%, *thought* it was boring to read about other people's **(2)** ______________ views online.

On food: 27% stated that they had posted successful recipes online to share with friends, while 13% admitted that they had read food blog posts and had watched demo videos but rarely cooked anything themselves. The majority of respondents reported that they had **(3)** ______________ the net for good recipes before having friends round for a meal.

On travel: The majority of people *thought* that the best way to research destinations and make **(4)** ______________ was via the net (55%) and a lot of people (43%) *enjoyed* sharing their experiences via blogs. Only 2% preferred to keep **(5)** ______________ about their travel in case their favorite places were over run with tourists.

On shopping: The vast majority of respondents (65%) said that they had bought their clothes online. 24% explained that they had looked at their favorite brands on the net, then went to the mall to try them on before they made a purchase. Only 11% claimed that they had bought mostly from **(6)** ______________.

On entertainment: 68% said that they had **(7)** ______________ or streamed most of their videos and movies from the net. 25% *preferred* to use the net mainly to catch up on TV programs. A minority of 7% declared that they rarely used the internet for entertainment.

On news: 59% *insisted* that they got the news from social media rather than from the newscasts or **(8)** ______________. 38% said that they looked at Twitter first when a news item broke and only 3% said that they had refused to use social media for news.

2 2.17 **Listen and check. Would the survey results be different in your country?**

GRAMMAR

1 **Which of the reporting verbs in the box can't you use to complete the statement below? Why not?**

admitted claimed explained insisted replied said suggested told

*13% ______________ that they **had read** blog posts and **had watched** demo videos.*

2 **In the reported statement in Exercise 1, the verb *read* is in the past perfect. Which sentence (*a*, *b*, *c*, or *d*) did people actually say?**

a "Yes, I was reading." **b** "Yes, I read." **c** "Yes, I've read." **d** "Yes, I'll read."

When you report speech, you usually move the tense back (e.g. present perfect becomes past perfect). True or false?

3 **Complete these sentences in direct speech. Use the reported statements highlighted in the survey results above to help you choose the correct form of the verb.**

a "Yes, I (read) *have read* recipes online."
b "Yes, I (surf) ______________ for good recipes before having friends for dinner."
c "Yes, I (stream) ______________ most of my videos and movies from the net."
d "Yes, I (get) ______________ the news from the net rather than from newscasts and newspapers."

Reported statements

"She's not there."
→ He **told** us that she **wasn't** there.
"I bought some new clothes."
→ She **said** that she**'d bought** some new clothes.

4 **Grammar Extra 9** page xi. Read the explanation and do the exercises.

SPEAKING

Find out how many people in the class ...

- are reading a novel right now.
- enjoy reading biographies and autobiographies.
- still listen to the same music that they did ten years ago.
- have a favorite place to read.
- buy and play music.
- prefer watching a movie to reading a book.
- have been to a concert recently.

LISTENING & VOCABULARY

1 2.18 **Listen to seven conversations. What are the people talking about in each one? Write *book*, *movie*, or *music*.**

1 *music*, 2 ...

2 **The table contains words and expressions relating to books, movies, and music from the seven conversations in Exercise 1. Complete the table with the correct heading (*Books* / *Movies* / *Music*) for each column.**

a ________	b ________	c ________
acting cinematography special effects tearjerker	album lyrics performing live techno track	bestseller can't put it down chapters difficult to get into

Add these words to the table. Some words go in more than one column. Add words of your own.

band blues classical dance director fantasy gig hip-hop a hit horror musical novel orchestra paperback plot premiere reggae science-fiction short story soundtrack stereo system storyline subtitles

3 2.19 **Listen to these extracts from movie soundtracks. What kind of movie do you think they go with? Choose from the list below.**

action movies comedies gangster movies horror movies love stories romantic comedies science-fiction movies spy movies thrillers war movies westerns

Work in groups. Think of some movies of each of the types above. Which types of movies do people in your group like best?

READING & GRAMMAR

1 **Read this report of an interview with Taylor Swift. What does she say about her fans, her song lyrics, and romance?**

In an online interview, Taylor Swift talked about how fame had changed her life. When the interviewer asked whether Taylor still invited fans into her home, she replied that she did. She said she liked to have small gatherings at her New York apartment because it helped her to bond with her fans on a more personal level. She felt it kept her down to earth and kept her life manageable.

When the interviewer asked her whether her life was still normal, Taylor said that it wasn't normal anymore. Taylor said that fame had changed everything. But she added that she keeps very close to her old friends and family, which helps her not to lose touch with reality.

Then they talked about her songs, which deal with the problems of everyday life. They asked Taylor what she felt about her critics. She replied that she didn't mind them. Some people said she was "brave" while others said she was "over-emotional". And when they asked her what her attitude to romance was now, she said that, since moving to New York, love and heartbreak — which used to be main themes in her music — had sort of faded to the background. They asked her what her current plans were and she replied that she was planning some new shows to promote her album.

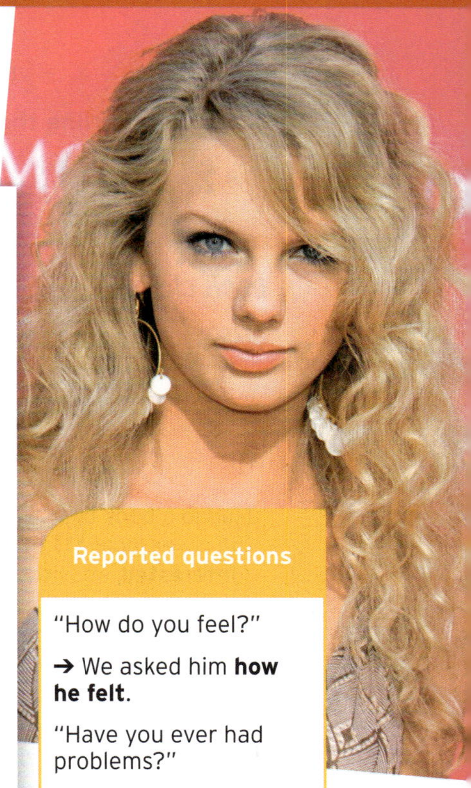

Reported questions

"How do you feel?"

→ We asked him **how he felt**.

"Have you ever had problems?"

→ We asked him **whether / if he had ever had** problems.

2 **What are the actual questions that are used in the interview? Underline the five reported questions in the report and rewrite them in direct speech.**

3 **Look at the examples in Exercise 2 and decide if the following statements are true or false when you report questions.**

a The tense usually moves back in a reported question (simple present → simple past).
b *Whether* or *if* are used to report *yes/no* questions. (*Did you go out?* → *She asked me if I'd gone out.*)
c The word order changes to subject + verb (*Who are you?* → *He asked me who I was.*).

4 **Pairwork Student A:** page i. **Student B:** page iv.

SPEAKING: ANECDOTE

1 2.20 **Listen to Alice talking about a movie she enjoyed. Read the questions and check (✓) the answers that are correct.**

a What's the title of the movie? **Forrest Gump.** ✓
b When and where did you see it?
The other night at the movie theater.
c Who's in it? **Tom Hanks, Robin Wright, and Sally Field.**
d Who directed it? **I can't remember.**
e What is it based on? **A true story.**
f What type of movie is it? **A thriller.**
g What do you particularly like about it?
The parts where he meets famous people.
h What was the soundtrack like? **Great.**
i What kind of ending does it have? **A happy ending.**
j Would you recommend this movie? **No, I wouldn't.**

Listen again and change the incorrect answers.

2 **You are going to tell your partner about a movie you enjoyed.**

- Ask yourself the questions in Exercise 1.
- Think about *what* to say and *how* to say it.
- Tell your partner about a movie you enjoyed.

VOCABULARY & SPEAKING

1 **Read and underline the correct alternatives in the sentences below.**

bookchoice.com

book choice Home Books Reviews Contact

We asked several people the question, "How do you choose a book to read?" Here are their replies.

I judge a book by its cover. If the cover looks **(1) <u>interesting</u> / interested**, I buy the book. Sometimes I'm lucky, and the book is good. And sometimes I'm **(2) disappointing / disappointed**.

I always read book reviews online, and when I read about a book that sounds **(3) interesting / interested**, I write it down in my notebook.

I don't take any risks and I always read books by authors I know. I get really **(4) exciting / excited** when one of my favorite authors puts out a new book, and I buy it immediately. This way I'm never **(5) disappointing / disappointed**.

I read the first page, and if it's **(6) boring / bored**, I don't buy the book. If I want to turn over the page and keep on reading, I buy the book.

It's easy – I never read fiction, but I'm **(7) fascinating / fascinated** by biographies of famous people. I find strong women in history particularly **(8) inspiring / inspired**.

I tend to choose books written by women. Women have a better feeling for characters and the relationships between them, and that's what I find **(9) interesting / interested** in a book.

2 2.21 **Listen and check your answers. How do you choose a book?**

3 **Add the adjectives in Exercise 1 to the table below.**

To describe how people feel	To describe the thing (or person) that causes the feeling
annoyed challenged confused exhausted relaxed tired worried	annoying challenging confusing exhausting relaxing tiring worrying

4 **Tell your partner how you're feeling today. Explain why. Choose words from the table in Exercise 3 or use your own ideas.**

Choose three other adjectives and say what makes you feel like this.

On Monday evenings, I feel exhausted. I work in a bar and it's very tiring.

PRONUNCIATION

1 **Say the words in the box and add them to the table.**

~~annoying~~ challenging disappointing entertaining exciting exhausting interesting overwhelming worrying

A: ■ ▪ ▪	
B: ▪ ■ ▪	annoying
C: ▪ ▪ ■ ▪	

2.22 **Listen, check, and repeat.**

2 **Underline the stressed syllable in each word.**

READING & VOCABULARY

1 **Look at the picture and read the synopsis of *Touching the Void* by Joe Simpson. What kind of book is it? Would you be interested in reading it? Why? / Why not?**

Look inside

Touching the Void

by Joe Simpson
★★★★☆ 1,610 customer reviews

Share

E-book	Hardcover	Paperback	Audible
$ 12.29	$ 19.86	$ 15.26	$ 17.17

Synopsis

Touching the Void is the heart-stopping account of Joe Simpson's terrifying adventure in the Peruvian Andes. A few days after Joe and his climbing partner, Simon, reach the summit of the remote Siula Grande, Simon staggers into Base Camp, exhausted and frostbitten, with news that Joe is dead.

Although this is a real-life account, it is a real page-turner. The technical information about mountain climbing is fascinating, and the stunning photos of the mountains give it authenticity, but it is the characters and plotline which make it more like a novel.

The story is told through Joe's eyes: the original disaster; what happens to Joe; and how the pair deals with the psychological traumas that resulted when Simon was forced into a terrible decision. It makes not only an epic story of survival, but an amazing tale of friendship.

2 **Read these reviews of *Touching the Void* from an online bookstore. How many stars do you think each person gave the book?**

a ☆☆☆☆☆ **Cliff-hanger**

by *S Cooke*
Format: Kindle Edition | **Verified Purchase**

Although the start of the book was a bit long and drawn out, by the time I reached chapter 5, I was hooked. Although I'm not a regular reader, and it took a long time to finish it, I am glad I did. If you are looking for an emotional "cliff-hanger" (sorry for the bad joke!) then this book is for you.

Comment

b ☆☆☆☆☆ **Astonishing!**

by *Mrs R Ramsden*
Format: Paperback | **Verified Purchase**

An astonishing story! It is as tense as any thriller and Joe's writing brings their struggles on the mountain to life. From my comfortable armchair, I can't begin to imagine what it must have been like for the two climbers. A tremendous read.

Comment

c ☆☆☆☆☆ **Repetitious and monotonous**

by *Charles Dickens*
Format: Kindle Edition | **Verified Purchase**

I didn't enjoy this book at all. The early part of the book is really monotonous; a repetitious account of ice and bad weather.

Comment

d ☆☆☆☆☆ **A bit too much!**

by *AVFC*
Format: Hardcover | **Verified Purchase**

I couldn't even bring myself to read all the way through. Too much tension for my taste. Perhaps it's just not my kind of book.

Comment

WRITING

Write a review of a book. Include the following information.

- The title of the book and the author.
- The central characters.
- The type of book.
- A summary of the plot (in the present tense).
- Where it takes place.
- What you liked or didn't like about the book.

LANGUAGE FOR LIFE

1 **Work in groups of three. Discuss the advantages and disadvantages of owning a car. Note down as many points as you can.**

2 2.23 **Listen to three friends having a discussion about owning a car. Do they mention any of the same points you noted down?**

3 **Work with a partner. Complete the conversation with one word in each space.**

Kayla: Hi, Ryan.
Julia: Hi, Ryan. What happened to you? You're late!
Ryan: Yes, I'm really sorry. I had to wait ages for a bus.
Julia: What's wrong with your car?
Ryan: I sold it! I **(1)** ___think___ there are too many cars in this city.
Julia: Well, that's true, **(2)** ________ a car is useful.
Ryan: I'm not so **(3)** ________ about that. The traffic's awful, and I can never find a parking space.
Kayla: But how are you going to get to work?
Ryan: By bicycle.
Kayla: **(4)** ________ you think bicycles are dangerous?
Ryan: Not really. They're certainly less dangerous for the environment.
Julia: Well, as far **(5)** ________ I'm concerned, *a car is essential*. I have to drive my kids to school.
Ryan: Your kids should walk to school. If you ask **(6)** ________, children don't get enough exercise.
Julia: I don't **(7)** ________ that's true! My kids do soccer, swimming, and tennis – and I need a car to get them there on time.

Kayla: I **(8)** ________ with Julia. I couldn't live without my car. I sometimes work in the evening, and I don't feel safe getting a bus late at night.
Ryan: OK, I see your point, **(9)** ________ aren't you worried about pollution?
Julia: Do you **(10)** ________ what I think? It's not my problem. I can't save the planet.
Ryan: I don't **(11)** ________. Everybody can do something!
Kayla: OK, OK, you're **(12)** ________! Now, let's change the subject. **(13)** ________ did you think of my new TV?
Julia: It's great, but I hope it's solar-powered!

Listen again and check your answers.

4 **Classify the highlighted expressions from the conversation in the following table.**

Ask for an opinion	Give an opinion	Agree with an opinion	Disagree with an opinion
Don't you think bicycles are dangerous?	*I think there are too many cars ...*	*Well, that's true, ...*	*I'm not so sure about that.*

2.24 **Listen and repeat the expressions. Copy the stress and intonation exactly.**

5 **Work in groups of three. Choose a topic below and note down all the advantages and disadvantages. Write a short conversation between three friends including some useful phrases from Exercise 4.**

petrol cars or electric cars   living abroad   living with your parents
using public transportation   working from home

Practice your conversation.

Life Skills: Negotiating
Borrowing the Car

1 **What are the golden rules of successful negotiating? Work with a partner and choose what you think are the key principles in this list.**

direct language
empathy
politeness
listening to the problems of others
brevity
no compromise
flexibility
aiming for a win/win

2 2.25 **Listen to the beginning of the conversation. Work with a partner and decide how best Rob could negotiate to get the car. Write out what he should say.**

3 2.26 **Listen to the rest of the conversation. Look at the list in Exercise 1. What went wrong for Rob? Discuss with your partner.**

4 **Role-play the situation between Rob and Rosa and come to a happy compromise.**

MACMILLAN LIFE SKILLS

9 Vocabulary Extra

Collocations

1 **Work with a partner. Decide which verbs combine most naturally with the nouns to form collocations.**

	action	advice	a comment	a decision	a mistake	an opinion
give	✗	✓				
make						
take						

Check your answers in the dictionary extracts for the nouns. Notice how strong collocations are in bold in the example sentences.

2 **Work with a partner. Decide if you agree or disagree with the following statements.**

a *Collocation* means the way that particular words regularly and naturally combine with each other. So *have an opinion* is a strong collocation, *own an opinion* is not.

b You should try to identify, record, and learn collocations that you find in English texts or in dictionary entries.

c Learning collocations will help you: (1) sound more natural; (2) be more precise; (3) improve your writing style.

3 **Underline the correct collocation in each of these dictionary examples.**

a **verb + noun**
*The students all **gave / provided / spoke** their opinions.*

b **adjective + noun**
*Professor Wright has a **big / high / large** opinion of your work.*

c **noun + noun**
*Despite our **disagreements / differences / distinctions** of opinion, we remained good friends.*

d **noun + preposition**
*What is your opinion **by / for / of** her latest novel?*

e **adverb + adjective**
*It now seems **highly / totally / completely** unlikely that the project will be finished on time.*

f **verb + adverb**
*Everyone spoke very **strongly / greatly / highly** of him.*

Check your answers in the dictionary extracts for *highly* and *opinion*.

4 **Use the collocation information in the dictionary extracts for *advice* and *mistake* to complete the questions.**

a Do you sometimes ask your boss or teacher __for__ advice?

b When was the last time you o________ advice to a friend?

c Are you more likely to a________ advice from your parents or your friends?

d Have you ever i________ somebody's advice and then regretted it?

e What's the most c________ mistake you've ever made?

Ask your partner the questions.

5 **Check your own dictionary. How does it show information about collocations?**

ac·tion /ˈækʃ(ə)n/ noun ★★★
1 [U] the process of doing something: *Police say they will **take** tough **action** against drug dealers.*

advice /ədˈvaɪs/ noun [U] ★★★ an opinion that someone gives you about the best thing to do in a particular situation: *Ask your father **for advice**.* ♦ *We are here to **give** people **advice about** health issues.* ♦ *I **took** his **advice** (=did what he advised) and left.* ♦ *She's **acting on** her lawyer's **advice**.*

Words often used with advice
*Verbs often used with **advice***
- **give, offer, provide** + ADVICE: give someone advice
- **ask for, seek** + ADVICE: ask for advice
- **accept, act on, follow, take** + ADVICE: do what someone advises
- **disregard, ignore, reject** + ADVICE: not do what someone advises

com·ment[1] /ˈkɑˌment/ noun [C/U] ★★★ a written or spoken remark giving an opinion: *I've had enough of your sarcastic comments.* ♦ *Did she **make** any **comment** about Eddie?*

de·ci·sion /dɪˈsɪʒ(ə)n/ noun ★★★
1 [C] a choice that you make after you have thought carefully about something: *The committee will **make a decision** by the end of the week.* ♦ *Have you **come to a decision** yet?* ♦ **a decision to do sth** *Mrs. Osman has announced her decision to retire.*

high·ly /ˈhaɪli/ adv ★★★
1 used before some adjectives to mean "very," or "very well": *It now seems **highly unlikely** that the project will be finished on time.* ♦ *She's a **highly educated** young woman.*
2 used for saying that someone or something is very good or very important: *a **highly valued** member of the staff* ♦ *Everyone we talked to **spoke** very **highly of** him.*

mis·take[1] /mɪˈsteɪk/ noun [C] ★★
1 something that you have not done correctly, or something you say or think that is not correct: *spelling/grammar mistakes*
2 something that you do that you later wish you had not done, because it causes a lot of problems: *You're **making a big mistake**.* ♦ **it would be a mistake to do sth** *It would be a mistake to think that the trouble is over.* ♦ **make the mistake of doing sth** *I made the mistake of inviting Jennifer to the party.*
PHRASE **by mistake** if you do something by mistake, you do it accidentally = BY ACCIDENT ≠ ON PURPOSE: *Oh no – I sent her the wrong letter by mistake.*

Words often used with mistake
*Adjectives often used with **mistake** (noun, sense 2)*
- **bad, big, costly, dreadful, fatal, serious, terrible** + MISTAKE: used about mistakes that have bad results

o·pin·ion /əˈpɪnjən/ noun [C] ★★★ the attitude that someone has toward something, especially about how good it is: *What is your **opinion of** her latest novel?* ♦ *Professor Wright **has a high opinion of** your work* (=thinks your work is good). ♦ *The students all **gave their opinions**.* ♦ *Despite our **differences of opinion**, we remained good friends.* ♦ *The book was a waste of time, **in my opinion**.* ♦ ***Public opinion** has turned against Senator McCormac in recent months.*

From the *Macmillan Essential Dictionary for Learners of American English*.

Review C

GRAMMAR

Grammar Extra pages vii-xii.

1 Underline the correct words.

a Has anyone ever **told you** / **told** that you have beautiful eyes?
b Do you mind **having** / **to have** your picture taken?
c Have you ever **promised to do** / **promised doing** something and then not done it?
d Do you enjoy **spending** / **spend** time alone on weekends?
e Did your parents ever tell you **not do** / **not to do** something, but you did it anyway?

Work with a partner. Ask and answer the questions.

2 Complete the text with the passive form of the verbs.

Yesterday two men (**1** arrest) _were arrested_ in St. Louis, after a bank manager (**2** rob) ________ . It (**3** believe) ________ that the thieves used a car that (**4** report) ________ stolen two days earlier. The car (**5** find) ________ abandoned several miles away. The two suspects (**6** take) ________ to the police station for questioning. The money (**7** not find) ________ yet. Anyone with information about the robbery (**8** ask) ________ to call St. Louis police.

3 Complete the story with the simple past or past perfect form of the verbs.

You'll never guess what happened to me last night! After finishing work, I (**1** go) _went_ to the gym, as usual. Then I went out to a restaurant with some clients. When it was time to go, I (**2** realize) ________ I (**3** leave) ________ my bag at the gym – with my keys in it! Unfortunately, my wife, Kerry (**4** not be) ________ at home because she (**5** go) ________ to Chicago for a meeting. Anyway, I went back to the gym, but it (**6** already close) ________ . So I went home. All the lights were off, so I (**7** decide) ________ to try and climb through the downstairs bathroom window, which was partly open. Just as I was trying to open the window, I (**8** see) ________ a light. It was two police officers. I explained that I (**9** lose) ________ my keys, but they wouldn't listen. They were just going to put me in the patrol car, when Kerry (**10** open) ________ the door. She (**11** get) ________ back early from her meeting, and (**12** be) ________ inside the house the whole time – watching a crime thriller on TV!

4 Underline the correct modals of deduction.

a Tim's plane has landed, but he's not here yet. He **can't** / **may** be stuck in Customs.
b There are some gray clouds in the sky. It **can** / **could** rain later.
c Everyone is leaving the office. It **may** / **must** be the end of the day.
d The lights in their apartment are all off. They're not answering the phone. They **can't** / **might** be at home.

5 Complete the sentences in reported speech.

a "I'm innocent!" The man told the police that he _was_ innocent.
b "I'm not a bank robber." He said that he ________ a bank robber.
c "I wasn't in town when the robbery happened." He claimed that he ________ in town when the robbery happened.
d "I have never seen Smith and Jones before." He added that he ________ Smith and Jones before.
e "I didn't rob the bank." He insisted that he ________ the bank.

VOCABULARY

1 Match the definitions with the words in the box.

desperate ~~hypocritical~~ insensitive obsessed photogenic unflattering

- **a** to describe someone pretending to be morally good but behaving in a way that shows that they are not sincere hypocritical
- **b** unable to stop thinking about something or someone
- **c** to describe someone who looks good in pictures
- **d** not noticing or caring about other people's feelings
- **e** making someone seem unpleasant or unattractive
- **f** needing or wanting something very much

2 Complete the sentences with the words in the box. There are two extra words.

arrested chase convicted court escorted sentenced shoplifted stolen ~~thief~~

- **a** The police caught the ___thief___ stealing a frozen chicken in the grocery store.
- **b** Police officers ______________ the gang to the police station.
- **c** Yesterday, three priceless paintings were ______________ from an art gallery in Denver.
- **d** Highway patrol have ______________ a sixteen-year-old boy after a ten-kilometer ______________ through Los Angeles.
- **e** The witness told the ______________ that she had seen the man holding the knife.
- **f** After a long trial, the judge ______________ the men to ten years in jail.

3 Underline the correct words.

Dear Mom and Dad,

We're having a great time here in Jamaica.

We're staying in a cabin on the **(1) sandy / southern** part of the island, overlooking the **(2) beach / white sands** of the beach below. We're **(3) surrounded / overlooking** by beautiful forests and have **(4) spectacular / towering** views of the mountains. Some of the beaches are very **(5) visible / popular** with tourists, but our little beach is hidden from the road, so it's completely **(6) unspoiled / packed**. I want to stay here forever!

Love, Alexis

4 Complete the words for features of a landscape.

- **a** a nc i ent r__ __ns
- **b** B__ddh__st t__mpl__
- **c** h__gh-r__s__ b__ __ld__ng
- **d** b__ __lt-__p skyl__n__
- **e** sn__ w-c__pp__d m__ __nt__ __n
- **f** w__t__rf__ll

PRONUNCIATION

1 Look at some words from Units 7-9. Say the words and add them to the table.

~~annoying~~ ~~celebrity~~ ~~classical~~ director dramatic embarrassing experience fantasy insensitive interviewed privacy suggested

A: ■ ■■ ■	annoying
B: ■■ ■ ■	classical
C: ■ ■■ ■ ■	celebrity

2 Underline the stressed syllable in each word.

▶ 2.27 **Listen, check, and repeat.**

READING & LISTENING

1 Read this newspaper article and decide which sentence (a, b or c) best summarizes the story.

- a Prince Harry is complaining that the paparazzi do not take enough pictures of him.
- b Prince Harry wishes that he could photograph the rich and famous.
- c Prince Harry does not like the paparazzi.

Daily News

Thursday, June 22, 2017

HARRY SPEAKS OUT

Prince Harry has spoken out about his hatred of some of the media. In particular, Harry has talked about the paparazzi who were chasing his mother, Princess Diana, on the night she was killed in a car crash in Paris. Her sons have always been unhappy that none of the paparazzi were arrested or charged with a criminal offence.

In a recent documentary, the prince talked about how his mother's life was dominated by the constant presence of journalists and photographers. He remembers that she could not leave the house or go to the gym without a group of journalists waiting for her and following her. These people often tried to insult her so that they could capture a picture of her getting mad at them. Once, when she was driving Harry and his older brother, William, to a friend's house, she was forced to stop the car because she was surrounded by photographers.

Harry recalls that she got out of the car to speak to them and when she came back she was crying. In the documentary, Harry said that as a young boy he had wanted to protect his mother, but felt unable to do so. Perhaps unsurprisingly, the youngest prince has been involved in disputes with the media himself. He once pushed a camera into a photographer's face when he came too close. He said he valued his private life and gets particularly upset when the media invade the privacy of his family and friends. He maintains that he is happy to be photographed and interviewed when he is carrying out his royal duties and on public occasions, but that he must be allowed to have a personal life.

2 Read the text again. Are these statements true or false?

- a Princess Diana's son is unhappy with some of the media.
- b Photographers were charged with a criminal offence after Princess Diana's death.
- c Harry wanted to protect his mother.
- d Harry once stole a camera.
- e A private life is important to Harry.
- f Harry does not want any photographs taken of him.

3 2.28 **Listen to a radio call-in show. Are the callers sympathetic to Harry?**

4 Listen again and underline the correct option to complete each sentence.

- a Megan completely **disagrees / agrees** with Prince Harry's views.
- b Megan thinks **all of us / none of us** would like to be watched all the time.
- c Charlie thinks the royal family **should / shouldn't** put up with intrusion.
- d The royal family **has to / doesn't have to** be popular.
- e Steven's view is **the same as / different to** Charlie's.
- f Steven thinks the royal family should be **respected / insulted**.
- g Bryn **does / doesn't** think Steve expressed his view clearly.

5 What do you think about Prince Harry's comments? Do you think he is entitled to privacy or not? Work in pairs. Discuss your opinion with a partner.

WRITING & SPEAKING

1 **Work with a partner. Look at a news reporter's notes for a story and compare them with her finished article.**

John Kronau (25) arrested by NY State Police

- Frightened cashier at Troy Savings Bank.
- Handed her note: "Don't be alarmed – this is bank deposit – please take money out of envelope, put in my account."
- Later said: "It was innocent joke."
- Added: "I've never been in trouble with police before."

25-year-old John Kronau **(1)** ___was___ arrested by the New York State Police after he **(2)** ________ frightened a bank cashier at Troy Savings Bank. Kronau handed the cashier **(3)** ________ note that read, "Don't be alarmed – this is **(4)** ________ bank deposit – please take the money out of **(5)** ________ envelope and put **(6)** ________ into my account." He later claimed that it **(7)** ________ been an innocent joke and added that he had never **(8)** ________ in trouble with **(9)** ________ police before.

Complete the finished article with the words in the box.

a	a	been	had	had	it	the	the	~~was~~

2 **Choose the best headline for the article.**

a BANK CASHIER ARRESTED **b** MAN ROBS BANK **c** JOKER HELD BY POLICE

3 **Look again at the notes, the finished article, and the headlines. Underline the correct words in these statements (a-c).**

a When you take notes you often **include** / **leave out** short words such as *a*, *the*, *be*, and *have*.
b You usually use **direct** / **reported** speech in notes and **direct** / **reported** speech in finished articles.
c In headlines you **include** / **leave out** short words such as *a*, *the*, *be*, and *have*.

4 **Work with your partner. Read the set of notes below and write up the finished article to appear in the next edition of *Internet News*. Write a headline for the story.**

- $5,000 stolen from grocery store (May 25), Dallas
- Local newspaper ran story, claimed thief took $7,000
- Thief called newspaper to complain and said: "Maybe store manager took extra $2,000"
- Staff at newspaper kept him busy on phone while police traced call.
- Arrested ten minutes later while still on phone talking to newspaper!

5 **Discuss the questions in small groups.**

a What amusing news stories have you heard recently?
b Should all news be heavy and serious, or is there a place for lightweight stories?
c Where do you get most of your news from – newspapers, TV, or the internet?
d In your opinion, what's the most important news story of the last week?

10 Childhood

READING & VOCABULARY

1 What is your earliest childhood memory? Ask a partner about theirs.

2 Read this extract from a book of childhood memories. Was the child helping her mom?

Glossary

flap (noun): a fast movement of something in the air
kid around (phrasal verb): behave in a silly way
settle (verb): something drops to the floor or bottom

My earliest memory is of helping my mom change the bed sheets. She used to try and flap the big sheet onto the big double bed and I would roll underneath every time. I thought it was really funny and I would laugh as the sheet settled on top of me. Mom found it funny to begin with and then she would start to get annoyed.

I guess she had lots of other things to do and I had all the time in the world for kidding around! Thinking about it, I wasn't really "helping", was I? But a strong memory of my entire childhood is that my mom was someone who loved me all the time, even when she was mad at me.

Work with a partner and think of three more endings to the following sentence:

A mom is someone who ...
picks you up when you fall over.

3 Underline the correct particle or preposition in these questions about childhood. Use a dictionary if necessary.

- a Who **brought** you **up** / **down**?
- b Who **told** you **off** / **apart** when you were bad?
- c Who **worried for** / **about** you when you went out at night?
- d Who **took care of** / **for** you when you were sick?
- e Who **tucked** you **in** / **away** at night?
- f Who **yelled at** / **for** you when they were angry with you?
- g Who **sat up** / **down** waiting for you to come home?
- h Who **cleaned up** / **out** after you had played with your toys?

Think about the different people who helped to take care of you in your own childhood – parents, older brothers and sisters, babysitters, etc. Answer the questions and compare your answers with your partner.

- **Grammar:** Defining relative clauses. Real conditionals. Indirect questions.
- **Vocabulary:** Phrasal verbs. Childhood. Verb-noun collocations. Proverbs. *make* and *let*.
- **Language for Life:** Describing objects

LISTENING

1 2.29 **Listen to some children defining four things from the list below. Which things do they talk about and in what order?**

a a dinosaur
b an iceberg
c a vet
d a robber
e a museum
f fall
g a desert
h a jungle

2 **Work with a partner. Imagine you are explaining other things from the list to a six-year-old child. Write down what you would say. Ask another pair of students to identify what you have defined.**

GRAMMAR

1 **Look at the children's definitions below showing the subject of the verb in the relative clauses. Answer the questions (1-3).**

a A person that (subject) helps (verb) animals.
b It's something that (subject) lived (verb) a very long time ago.

1 In which definition can you replace the relative pronoun *that* with *which*?
2 In which definition can you replace the relative pronoun *that* with *who*?
3 Is it possible to leave out the relative pronouns in these definitions? Why?/Why not?

Defining relative clauses

an adult who **takes care of you**

a child (that) **you take care of**

a toy which **makes a noise**

a toy (that) **you play with**

2 **Work with your partner. Read the definitions (a-d) of words to do with childhood and follow the instructions (1-3).**

a A *truant* is a student who stays away from school without permission.
b A *bib* is a piece of cloth that protects babies' clothes when they are eating.
c A *pacifier* is a plastic object which you put in a baby's mouth to stop the baby from crying.
d A *nanny* is a person who you employ to take care of your children.

1 Underline the relative clauses in each definition.
2 Identify the subject and the verb in each relative clause.
3 Decide which relative pronouns you need to keep and which ones you can leave out.

What is the translation of these relative pronouns in your language?

3 **Pairwork Student A:** page ii **Student B:** page v

4 **Work with a partner. Put the words in the correct order to make questions about your memories of childhood. Then discuss questions 1 and 2.**

What can you remember about ...

a to / the school / that / went / you ?
the school that you went to?
b played / the toys / with / you / that ?
c that / you / to / invited / the parties / were ?
d the books / were / in / which / interested / you ?
e about / that / the things / you / worried / were ?
f the things / dream / used to / of / that / you ?

1 What type of word does each question end with?
2 Can you leave out the relative pronouns *which* and *that* in these questions? Why?/Why not?

Work with your partner. Ask and answer the questions (a-f).

5 **Grammar Extra 10, Part 1** page xiii. Read the explanation and do the exercises.

READING

1 Which of the following statements about childhood do you agree with? Discuss with a partner.

- a School days are the best days of your life.
- b Children don't have as much fun these days as they did 40 or 50 years ago.
- c There is too much emphasis on tests and exam results these days.
- d Children are becoming more independent at a young age.
- e It's good for children to be bored sometimes.
- f Parents should never lie to their children.

2 Read this text and choose the best title.

Kids Need To Play | Schools of Tomorrow | Chinese Education

mblog.com

M blog

Thursday, May 25, 2017

I grew up in the United States in the 1950s and I consider myself lucky. It was a time when kids were given a lot of freedom. We went to school, but it wasn't the big deal it is today. Teachers didn't watch over us all the time, and if they saw us behaving badly, they rarely intervened. We wrestled in the dirt, climbed trees in the woods, and had snowball wars in winter – none of which would be allowed today. Out of school, we had our chores, and some of us had part-time jobs such as paper rounds (which gave us a sense of maturity and money of our own) but, most of the time, we were free – free to play for hours each day after school, all day on weekends, and all summer long. Homework was non-existent in elementary school and minimal in high school. There seemed to be an understanding that children need lots of time and freedom to play — if children play, they will develop a wide range of skills.

How times have changed. Just today, the Education Secretary has announced plans to make school days longer and school holidays shorter. The hope is that if students are in school longer, it will raise test scores

to the level of those in China, Singapore, and other East Asian nations. But things may be changing in those Asian countries. The Chinese Ministry of Education thinks children should have less time in school and less homework. The report also said that test scores should be focused on less. Because students spend nearly all their time studying, they don't have much time to be creative or follow their passions. They don't develop physical and social skills in the same way as kids did in the past. In addition, some schoolchildren these days suffer from extraordinarily high levels of anxiety, depression, and stress disorders, which appear to be linked to academic pressure. Unless educators think again, students will continue to miss out on valuable play time.

3 According to the article which version of these statements is correct?

- a The author is in favor of **free play / child labor**.
- b When the author was young, teachers **frequently** / **rarely** intervened.
- c **Climbing trees** / **Doing homework** wouldn't be allowed today.
- d The author thinks part-time jobs give children **a sense of maturity** / **a feeling of stress**.
- e The Education Secretary wants to make **school days** / **holidays** shorter.
- f Academic pressure can lead to **anxiety** / **happiness**.

What were your school days like? Do you think there was too much work and not enough play? Discuss with a partner.

PRONUNCIATION

1 2.30 **Listen to the words and identify the silent letter in each group.**

a	know	knee	knife
	Silent letter = k		
b	white	hour	ghost
c	doubt	debt	bomb
d	castle	listen	often
e	whose	wrist	sword
f	psychologist	pneumonia	psychiatrist

2 **Listen again and repeat.**

GRAMMAR

1 **Read this extract from the article on page 94.**

Unless educators think again, students will continue to miss out on valuable play time.

Complete the second sentence so that it has the same meaning as the extract above.

If educators ________________ *think again, students will continue to miss out on valuable play time.*

2 **Read these rules about real conditional sentences. Are they true or false?**

a Real conditional sentences have two clauses: an *if*-clause and a main clause.
b They talk about "real" or possible situations including threats, warnings, and promises.
c You usually use a present tense in the *if*-clause – you never use *will*.
d You usually use *will*, *can*, *might*, etc. or an imperative form in the main clause.
e *Unless* means the same as *if ... not*.

Real conditionals

If it**'s** fine on Sunday, we**'ll go** for a picnic.

If you **want** to join us, **bring** some food.

Jon **won't come** unless you **ask** him.

unless = if ... not

3 **Work with a partner. Read the following sentences said by a parent to a child and discuss the meanings. Underline the correct alternatives.**

a If **you're** / **you'll be** very good, I might buy you an ice cream cone.
b If **you fall off** / **you'll fall off** that wall, don't come crying to me.
c If **you'll call** / **you're calling** your friends this evening, don't stay on the phone too long.
d **If** / **Unless** you hurry up, you'll be late for school.
e If **you haven't finished** / **you've finished** your homework, you can't watch TV.
f If **you finished** / **you are finishing** your dinner, you can leave the table.
g **If** / **Unless** you're going to stay out late, take a front door key.
h If **you're going to play** / **you'll play** that awful music, shut your door.

What age (0-18) do you think the child would be if a parent was saying these things?

4 **Grammar Extra 10, Part 2** page xiii. Read the explanation and do the exercises.

VOCABULARY & SPEAKING

1 **Correct the statements (a-f).**

a If the boss ~~will be~~ is away, nobody will do any work.
b If you will get something easily, you won't be sorry to lose it.
c Unless you will consider something carefully, you might fail.
d Unless you will concentrate, you won't succeed.
e If you will fail the first time, you might not want to try again.
f Unless you will make an effort, you won't succeed.

1 You snooze, you lose.
2 No pain, no gain.
3 Once bitten, twice shy.
4 Easy come, easy go.
5 Look before you leap.
6 When the cat's away, the mice will play.

Match each statement (a-f) to a common English proverb (1-6).

2 **Work with a partner. Think of other proverbs you have in your own language(s). How would you say them in English using *If* ... or *Unless* ...?**

LISTENING & GRAMMAR

1 2.31 **Listen to a TV show about bringing up children and choose the best definition for pushy parents.**

a Parents who are very liberal and give their children lots of freedom.
b Parents who are very ambitious for their children to be the best, whatever the cost.
c Parents who are very strict and don't allow their children to play or have friends.

2 Listen again and underline the correct alternative.

a George and Rachel **agree** / **disagree** about how to bring up their daughter.
b Hayley is **four** / **five** years old.
c Rachel wants Hayley to be a **rock** / **movie** star.
d Hayley has singing lessons and acting classes every **week** / **summer**.
e On weekends Hayley goes to **parties** / **auditions**.
f George thinks his wife is **obsessed** / **reasonable**.
g **George** / **Rachel** is the "pushy parent."

3 The studio audience asked George and Rachel some questions. Look at the answers.
Write G if you think it's George's opinion and R if you think it's Rachel's.

a How does Hayley feel?
"She enjoys life." ☐
"She's too young to know." ☐
b What are you going to do when Hayley starts school?
"Continue doing auditions." ☐
"Stop doing auditions. Our child isn't a business." ☐
c Are you depriving Hayley of a normal childhood?
"Yes." ☐ "No." ☐
d Do you have any other children and how are they affected?
"Yes, our son misses his mom." ☐
"Yes, our son is proud of his little sister." ☐
e How stressful is it to be a movie star?
"Very stressful." ☐
"We can cope." ☐

2.32 **Listen and check.**

4 The questions in Exercise 3 are direct questions, but the audience actually asked indirect questions. Complete their indirect questions using the question frames below.

a Do you know ... *how Hayley feels?*
b Can you tell me ...
c Do you think ...
d Could you tell me ...
e Do you have any idea ...

Indirect questions

How **does she feel**? →
Do you know how **she feels**?

Is she happy? →
Can you tell me **if/ whether she's** happy?

2.33 **Listen and check.**

5 Work with a partner. Answer these questions about the construction of indirect questions.

a Do you use *do/does/did* in indirect questions?
b Is the word order (subject + verb) the same as in affirmative sentences?
c Do you use *if/whether* for *yes/no* questions?

6 Work with your partner. Put the ends of these indirect questions in the correct order.

a Do you think ... were / your parents / pushy parents ?
your parents were pushy parents?
b Do you know ... in the same city / if / were born / your parents ?
c Do you have any idea ... your parents / how / met ?
d Do you think ... children / too much time / spend / on digital devices / these days ?
e Can you tell me ... are / what / your ambitions for your children ?

Ask your partner the questions.

VOCABULARY

1 **Rewrite the sentences using *make* or *let*.**

a I'm not **forcing her to do** anything against her will. → I'm not …
b She's a kid – **allow her to play, allow her to have** friends. → She's a kid …

Which comment did Rachel make? Which comment did George make?

Choose 1 or 2 to complete the rule.

The correct verb pattern for *make* and *let* is:
1 *make/let* + somebody + *to*-infinitive.
2 *make/let* + somebody + infinitive without *to*.

2 **Complete the sentences with two words from the box so that they make sense. You can use the negative.**

let made me us

a My parents ___let me___ wear jewelry to school.
b My parents ______________ do the dishes.
c Our teachers ______________ use their first names.
d My sister never ______________ borrow her clothes.
e My parents ______________ keep my room clean.
f My brother sometimes ______________ borrow his MP3 player.
g My parents ______________ dye my hair.
h Our gym teacher ______________ play outside in bad weather.

How many sentences are true for you? Change the sentences into questions. Ask a partner.

Did your parents let you wear jewelry to school?

No, they didn't. Did yours?

SPEAKING: ANECDOTE

1 2.34 **Listen to Rafi talking about an activity he used to do when he was a child. Underline the correct information.**

a What was the activity?
Martial arts. / Art classes.
b Why did you choose that activity?
I liked kung fu movies. / My friends did it.
c Was it your idea or your parents' idea?
It was my parents' idea. / My idea.
d Did you enjoy it? **No, I hated it. / Yes, I was obsessed with it.**
e How often did you do it? **Once a week. / Two or three times a week.**
f Where did you do it? **At a gym. / At school.**
g How did you get there and back?
My parents drove me there. / I rode my bike.
h Do you still do it now? **Yes, I do. / No, I gave it up.**
i Would you encourage your own children to do the same thing? **No, absolutely not! / Yes, definitely.**

2 **You are going to tell your partner about an activity you did when you were a child.**

- Ask yourself the questions in Exercise 1.
- Think about *what* to say and *how* to say it.
- Tell your partner about your activity.

LANGUAGE FOR LIFE

1 2.35 **Read and listen to four people describing their favorite gadget. Match the conversations (a-d) with the pictures (1-4).**

a

A: It's one of those things you use to massage your head and it feels amazing.
B: What does it look like?
A: It's made of metal and it looks like a big spider with long legs.

b

C: It's a kind of fan that sprays water in your face.
D: What's it for?
C: It's for cooling yourself down when it's really hot.

c

E: Have you seen this fantastic gadget?
F: What do you do with it?
E: You use it to peel a pineapple. You put it on top of the pineapple and turn it until it reaches the bottom. Then you pull it out, and you have a perfect cylinder of pineapple.

d

G: Oh, no, there's an enormous spider in the bathtub! Go and get the spider catcher.
H: What does it look like?
G: It's round with a long handle.

1

2
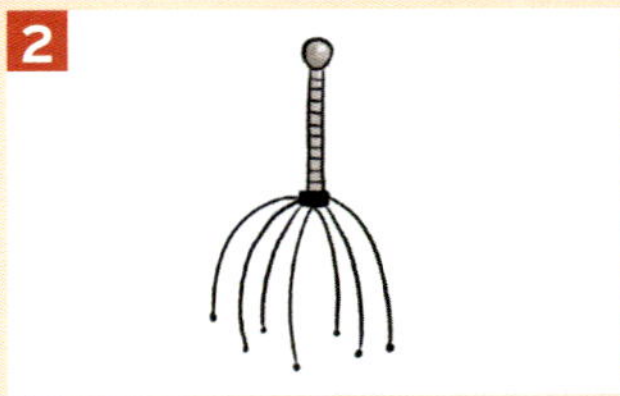

3

4
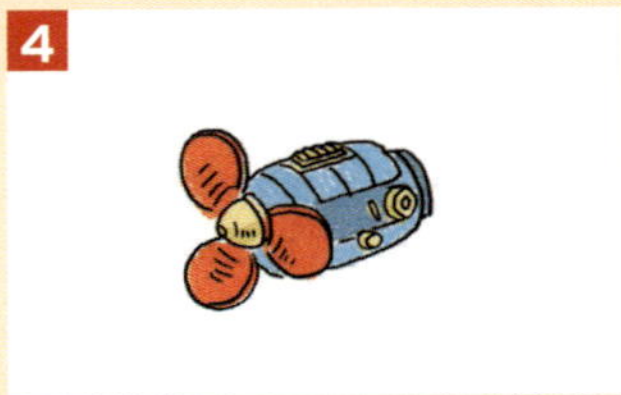

2 **Complete the table with the highlighted phrases from the conversations in Exercise 1.**

Purpose: what's it for	Appearance: what it looks like	Material: what it's made of
a *It's one of those things you use to massage your head.*	d It looks like a big spider.	f It's made of ______
b It's for ______	e It's ______	
c You use it to ______		

2.36 **Listen and repeat the expressions.**

3 **Look at the words and phrases in the box. Find three more ways to complete each of the useful phrases *b*, *c*, *e*, and *f* in Exercise 2. Use your dictionary if necessary.**

cardboard light the gas long and thin plastic recharge your cell phone rectangular ~~removing stains~~ small and square stainless steel ~~storing things~~ straightening your hair unblock toilets

b *It's for removing stains / storing things / ...*

4 **Describe your own favorite gadgets to your partner.**

Life Skills: Giving Feedback
Parenting

1 2.37 **Listen to two parents of 3-year-olds talking about giving feedback to their child. Which one had the most positive outcome? Why?**

2 **Complete this list of tips for giving feedback with words from the box.**

at the right time effect positive behavior possible

Giving feedback should ...

- be about **(1)** ______ not personality.
- describe the **(2)** ______ of the person's behavior on you.
- be **(3)** ______, so don't delay for too long.
- be as specific as **(4)** ______.
- be **(5)** ______ and clear.

3 **Discuss:**

How do/did your parents give you feedback? Is/Was it effective?

How different is it with kids today?

MACMILLAN LIFE SKILLS

10 Vocabulary Extra

Word families

1 **Work with a partner. Which word in each list does not exist? Cross it out.**

a disqualify misuse overcooked undernational
b unused misqualify undercooked unemployment
c inadvisable overnationalistic reusable unqualified

Check your ideas in the dictionary extracts. Check (✓) the words you know.

2 **Look again at the dictionary extracts. How do the prefixes in the box change the meanings of the base words?**

dis mis over re un/in under

Match each prefix with its approximate meaning (a-f).

a not = ______________
b too much = ______________
c wrongly = ______________
d no longer = ______________
e again = ______________
f not enough = ______________

3 **Guess the meaning of the following words.**

a discontinue
b misprint
c oversleep
d redo
e unaware
f underpay

Check your answers in your own dictionary.

4 **Copy the table and complete it by putting the words from the dictionary extracts in the appropriate columns according to their word class.**

Verbs	Adjective	Noun	Noun (person)
advise	*advisable*	*advice*	*adviser*
cook			
employ			
	national		
qualify			
use			

Match the parts of speech (a-d) with the lists of typical suffixes (1-4).

a verb
b adjective
c noun
d noun (person)

1 able (ible), al, ed, ful, ic, less
2 age, er, ing, ion, ism, ity, ment
3 ee, er (or)
4 ify, ize (ise)

5 **Choose a word from Exercise 4 to complete each sentence.**

a I'm not a very good (cook) ______________ . I don't even know how to boil an egg.
b I hate the (national) ______________ feelings that events like the Olympic Games encourage.
c Everyone needs a financial (advise) ______________ . They can save you a lot of money.
d I think that experience is more important than a lot of (qualify) ______________ .
e I try to (use) ______________ any water bottles that I buy instead of just throwing them away.
f I've never been (employ) ______________ . Since I started working, I haven't stopped.

Are any of the sentences true for you?

6 **Check your own dictionary. How does it present word families?**

Word family: advise
Words in the same family as **advise**
- **advice** *n*
- **advisable** *adj*
- **adviser** *n*
- **advisory** *adj*
- **inadvisable** *adj*

Word family: cook
Words in the same family as **cook**
- **cooked** *adj*
- **overcooked** *adj*
- **cooking** *n*
- **undercooked** *adj*

Word family: employ
Words in the same family as **employ**
- **employed** *adj*
- **employment** *n*
- **employer** *n*
- **unemployed** *adj*
- **unemployment** *n*
- **employee** *n*

Word family: national
Words in the same family as **national**
- **nation** *n*
- **nationalize** *v*
- **nationalism** *n*
- **nationality** *n*
- **international** *adj*
- **nationalized** *adj*
- **nationalistic** *adj*
- **multinational** *adj,n*

Word family: qualify
Words in the same family as **qualify**
- **qualification** *n*
- **qualified** *adj*
- **disqualified** *adj*
- **qualifier** *n*
- **unqualified** *adj*
- **disqualify** *v*

Word family: use
Words in the same family as **use**
- **usage** *n*
- **used** *adj*
- **useful** *adj*
- **useless** *adj*
- **reusable** *adj*
- **user** *n*
- **unused** *adj*
- **misuse** *n, v*
- **reuse** *v*

From the *Macmillan Essential Dictionary for Learners of American English.*

11 Age

LISTENING & VOCABULARY

1 Work with a partner. Think about an older person you admire.

a How long have you known them?
b What is special about them?
c What one thing would you like to learn from them?

Are your answers similar?

2 2.38 **Read and listen to a radio show about two amazing older people. Match each one to the presenter's comments.**

a You look like someone fifty years younger!
b You must have been completely exhausted!

1

2

Jen: Morning everyone, and welcome to People's Hour. Today, we are talking about age. Let's meet two extraordinary people who are really living life to the max! Firstly, Georgina Harwood: Georgina, you may be 100, but you could just as **(1) unfortunately / easily / obviously** look like someone fifty years younger!

Georgina: Good morning, Jen!

Jen: Now, Georgina, tell us what you did to celebrate your 100th birthday?

Georgina: So, I decided to do a sky dive. I wasn't sure anyone would come and support me, but **(2) easily / luckily / unfortunately** for me, 15 members of my extended family came to watch.

Jen: How did you prepare for the jump?

Georgina: Well, I prepared very **(3) unluckily / completely / thoroughly**. I exercised every day for three months before the dive. And I listened very **(4) completely / carefully / easily** to my instructor.

Jen: Have you always been a risk-taker?

Georgina: I guess so. If I wasn't a risk-taker, I wouldn't be here today – it keeps me stimulated and active.

Jen: And how did you feel during the dive itself?

Georgina: I felt **(5) completely / fortunately / luckily** free and totally relaxed. Of course, it did help being held firmly in the arms of my lovely instructor Dave!

Jen: Any regrets?

Georgina: None, but I thought if I didn't do it, I would **(6) absolutely / probably / carefully** spend the rest of my life regretting it.

Jen: Thank you, Georgina. Now, my next guest is on the line from Japan, Mr Yuichura Miura. Yuichura, please tell us about your big achievement?

Yuichura: Hello, Jen, I can proudly say that I am the oldest person to have climbed Mount Everest.

Jen: And how old were you when you did it?

Yuichura: I was 80, and that was several years ago.

Jen: Congratulations! But you must have felt **(7) unfortunately / fortunately / completely** exhausted afterwards?

Yuichura: Yes, I was tired, but if I hadn't been **(8) fairly / completely / carefully** fit, I don't think I would have made it.

Jen: "Fairly fit" must be an understatement, Yuichura! After climbing Everest, did you take a well-deserved break from climbing?

Yuichura: Yes, I did for a while. My wife **(9) completely / really / particularly** wants me to give up climbing for good. **(10) Luckily / Personally / Absolutely**, I am keen to continue for as long as I can. If I stop, I might never climb again!

3 Underline the appropriate "attitude" verbs.

4 Listen again and check.

- **Grammar:** Unreal conditionals. Wishes and regret.
- **Vocabulary:** Adverbs of attitude/manner. Age.
- **Language for Life:** On the telephone

PRONUNCIATION

1 **Practice saying the attitude adverbs in the box and then add them to the table. Underline the stressed syllable.**

~~actually~~ apparently definitely fortunately incredibly naturally
obviously positively practically predictably regularly surprisingly

A: ■ ■ ■	actually
B: ■ ■ ■ ■	
C: ■ ■ ■ ■	

2 2.39 **Listen, check, and repeat.**

VOCABULARY

1 **Look at this simple sentence structure. In which position (1-4) is it possible to put the adverb of manner *carefully*?**

subject verb object
(1) Georgina **(2)** listened to **(3)** the instructor **(4)**.

2 **Rewrite these sentences in the correct order.**

a prepared / very / I / thoroughly
b free / completely / felt / I
c You / exhausted / must / have / felt / completely
d really / She / wants me / climbing / give up / to

GRAMMAR

1 **Work with your partner. Look at the unreal conditional sentence about Georgina Harwood. Check (✓) the "real situation" (*a*, *b*, or *c*) that the sentence is based on.**

"If I wasn't a risk-taker, I wouldn't be here today ..."

a She's here today. She is a risk-taker.
b She wasn't here. She wasn't a risk-taker.
c She will be here. She will be a risk-taker.

Underline the correct alternative.

When you want to talk about unreal or imaginary situations in the present:
use (1) **the simple past** / ***would* + infinitive** in the *if*-clause;
use (2) **the simple past** / ***would* + infinitive** in the main clause.

Unreal conditionals (1)

Real situation:
I **can't** sing. I'**m not** in a band.
time (present) = tense (present)

Unreal or imaginary situation:
If I **could** sing, I'**d be** in a band.
time (present) ≠ tense (past)

if-clause: simple past

Main clause: *would/wouldn't* + infinitive

2 **Write unreal conditional sentences based on the real situations below. Start each sentence with *If* ...**

a I don't have a car. I can't drive to work.
If I had a car, I'd be able to drive to work.
b I can't cook. I don't invite my friends over for dinner.
c I don't live abroad. I see my family very regularly.
d I go out every night. I'm always tired.
e I don't have time. I don't do my English homework.
f I have to learn English. I can't learn another language.

Are any of these conditional sentences true for you? Discuss with your partner.

3 **Pairwork Student A:** page iii **Student B:** page vi

READING

1 **Work in groups. Look at the picture, but don't read the poem. Invent an identity for the person in the picture.**

- **a** What's her name?
- **b** How old is she?
- **c** Where does she live?
- **d** What's her family background?
- **e** What has she done in her life?
- **f** Is she happy?

Compare your ideas with other people in the class.

Glossary

PCT: Pacific Crest Trail

whine (verb): make a complaining noise

nettle (noun): wild plant with pointed leaves that sting when touched

If…

If I could live my life over again
I would chill out.
I'd be less sensible, less careful.
I would take more risks.
I would take more trips and climb more mountains,
Dive from the sky and fly down volcanos on a tray.
I would drink and eat more.
I would leave a bad job in the city and roam wild.
I would hike the PCT, hear more birdsong, and soak up the landscape.
I would notice the good, not pick out the bad.
And take ten deep breaths at the beginning of each day.
I would live in the moment, every moment.
I would be more carefree. I would think more of others
but Worry less what others thought.
I would say "I love you" more and "sorry" too.
I would chat more and snapchat less.
There would be more time for fun and less for fear.
I would take more time to stand and stare,
I would laugh and joke and smile, not frown or whine.
I would seize the day and grasp the nettle and all those other things
You're meant to do.
I would walk barefoot. I would pick more flowers.

2 2.40 **Read and listen to the poem and decide whether it fits the character you have invented. How does the person in the poem feel about her life?**

GRAMMAR

1 Complete these sentences for a person expressing regrets. Use the words in the box.

adventurous ~~anxious~~ enjoy fun over risks sensible seriously

a I wish I'd been less ___anxious___.
b I wish I'd been more ___________ .
c I wish I'd taken more ___________ .
d If only I'd had more ___________ .
e I wish I hadn't been so ___________ .
f I wish I hadn't taken life so ___________ .
g If only I'd done more of the things I ___________ .
h I wish I had my life to live ___________ .

Wishes and regrets

Facts (present/past):

I **can't swim**. **I didn't take** lessons at school.

Wishes or regrets (past / past perfect):

I wish **I could** swim.

If only **I had taken** lessons at school.

2 Write the corresponding fact for each regret expressed in Exercise 1.

a *I was anxious.*

Underline the correct alternative.

a When you want to express a wish or regret about a present fact, you use a **present** / **past** tense after *wish* / *if only*.
b When you want to express a wish or regret about a past fact, you use a **past** / **past perfect** tense after *wish* / *if only*.

3 Work with a partner. Write a wish or regret for each of these facts.

a I couldn't go to the latest Coldplay gig.
I wish / if only I'd been able to go to the latest Coldplay gig.
b I didn't learn English at school.
c I'm not married.
d I don't know how to play chess.
e I can't play the guitar.
f I'm going on a training course next week.
g I'm studying for exams right now.
h I couldn't swim when I was a child.

Are any of the facts, wishes, or regrets true for you? Discuss with your partner.

4 **Grammar Extra 11, Part 1** page xv. Read the explanation and do the exercises.

SPEAKING

1 Work with your partner. Think about the possible story behind each of these pictures. Talk about each of those situations. Use: *I wish* ... or *If only* ...

a

b

c

d

e

f

2 Have you made any bad decisions today/this week/ this year/in your life so far? Talk about them with your partner.

I wish I hadn't gone to bed so late last night. I feel really tired today.

READING & SPEAKING

1 **Imagine you could go back in time and you met your 15-year-old self. What would you say to them? What advice would you give? Discuss with a partner.**

2 **Read the article about Peter Emshwiller, who has used clever video technology to "interview" a younger version of himself. Why is the younger Peter disappointed?**

An Interview with Yourself

If you could really talk to your younger self, what would you say? When he was 18, Peter Emshwiller filmed himself asking his older self questions. He also recorded all the possible reactions to the questions, from polite nods to joy, sadness, annoyance, surprise and horror. Forty-eight years later, Emshwiller, now 66, created a film where he answers the questions asked by his 18-year-old self. The film is called *Later That Same Life*. It's a fascinating film.

One of the first questions the Young Peter asked was whether his future self was "exceedingly rich". Old Peter just laughed and shook his head. Young Peter also wanted to know how things had gone for his family, and in a moving moment, Old Peter simply advised his younger self to spend as much time as he could with his family, especially his father. When he was asked whether he was now a superstar, Older Peter said "no". In fact, Old Peter became a little defensive, saying that he didn't always have to live up to his dreams. Maybe Old Peter was feeling defensive because he felt disappointed, too. If he had taken a different path, perhaps he would have become a superstar. He would have pleased his younger self.

3 2.41 **Listen to the last few minutes of the interview and write the final paragraph of the article, reporting what final questions young Peter asked his older self.**

4 **Work in small groups to write the questions for an interview with yourself in 40 years' time.**

GRAMMAR

1 Work with a partner. Look at the unreal conditional sentence from the article on page 104. Check (✓) the real situation (*a*, *b*, or *c*) that the sentence is based on.

If he had taken a different path, perhaps he would have become a superstar.

a He doesn't take a different path. He doesn't become a superstar.
b He didn't take a different path. He didn't become a superstar.
c He won't take a different path. He won't become a superstar.

Underline the correct alternative.

When you want to talk about "unreal" or imaginary situations in the past: use (1) **the past perfect / would +** have **+ past participle** in the *if*-clause; use (2) **the past perfect / would +** have **+ past participle** in the main clause.

> **Unreal conditionals (2)**
>
> **Real situation:**
>
> I **didn't have** a map.
>
> I **got** lost.
>
> time (past) = tense (past)
>
> **Unreal or imaginary situation:**
>
> If I'**d had** a map, I **wouldn't have gotten** lost.
>
> time (past) ≠ tense (past perfect)
>
> *if*-clause: past perfect
>
> Main clause: *would/wouldn't* + *have* + past participle

2 Write unreal conditional sentences based on the real situations below. Start each sentence with *If* ...

a I didn't see you yesterday. I didn't say hello.
If I'd seen you yesterday, I'd have said hello.
b I stayed up late last night. I overslept this morning.
c I couldn't find a parking space. I arrived late for the class.
d My sister traveled around the world. She met her future husband.
e I didn't learn to drive when I was 18. I didn't have a car in college.
f It rained yesterday. I didn't go for a walk.

Are any of these conditional sentences true for you? Discuss with your partner.

3 Grammar Extra 11, Part 2 page xv. Read the explanation and do the exercises.

READING & SPEAKING

1 Work with a partner. Look at these four key words from three different stories. What do you think each story is about?

1 parking garage, car, money, dropped
2 laptop, posting, kissing, social media
3 restaurant, courses, wrong, check(2X)

2 Read and complete the texts by matching the words from Exercise 1 to each story. Discuss what you would have done in each situation.

a

I was walking through the shared **(1)** *parking garage* at work the other day when I saw a pile of 50 dollar bills on the ground beside a large black luxury car. The **(2)** __________ was a top of the range model with a personalized license plate. It looked like it belonged to some billionaire or a mafia boss or something. If the **(3)** __________ had been **(4)** __________ by the owner of the car, I figured he probably wouldn't notice, as he was obviously really rich. There was no one else in the parking garage.

b

I made a shocking discovery last night. I was at my **(5)** __________, with my social media page open, when I noticed a **(6)** __________ from a guy in my group of ex-college friends. That was OK, but the problem is that in the background of one of the photos from their recent boys' trip, I saw my best friend's boyfriend **(7)** __________ another girl. My friend is not on Facebook in fact she's not on **(8)** __________, so she may not see the picture or find out about her boyfriend unless someone tells her.

c

Ed and I went to our local Chinese **(9)** __________ the other day with a couple of friends. We had a lovely meal with three **(10)** __________, drinks, and coffees. When we got the **(11)** __________ it seemed very reasonable, and Ed paid. It was only when we got home and I looked at the check that we realized that we had been given the **(12)** __________ **(13)** __________. It was meant for the table next to ours and was about half the amount it should have been.

▶ 2.42 **Listen and find out what the people did. Do you think they did the right thing?**

LANGUAGE FOR LIFE

1 Look at the useful phrases (1-7) for telephoning. In each case, cross out the phrase that is unusual or incorrect.

1 Hello. / Good morning. / ~~Speak me~~.
2 Is (name) there? / I'd like to speak to (name), please. / Is there (name)?
3 Are you (name)? / Is this (name)? / Who's calling, please?
4 Just a moment, please. I'll try to put you through. / Hold on, I'll go and get her. / One instant.
5 I am me. / It's me. / (name) here.
6 What are you up to later? / What do you do later? / Are you available later on today?
7 I'll look forward to seeing you tomorrow. / To tomorrow. / See you tomorrow.

2 Read two phone calls made by Phil Jones: one to his friend, Maddy, and the other to his bank. Complete each conversation with the most appropriate useful phrases from Exercise 1.

Conversation A

Janet: **(1)** ________________
Phil: Oh, hi. **(2)** ________________
Janet: **(3)** ________________
Phil: Yes. Hello, Janet. How are you?
Janet: Fine, thanks. **(4)** ________________
Maddy: Hello.
Phil: Hi! **(5)** ________________
Maddy: Hi there! What have you been doing?
Phil: Oh, just working. Listen, I can't talk now. **(6)** ________________
Maddy: I have to work this evening, but I thought we could go to the movies tomorrow.
Phil: OK, I'll come over about seven.
Maddy: **(7)** ________________
Phil: Bye.

Conversation B

Receptionist: **(1)** ________________ Northminster Bank. Can I help you?
Phil: Yes, **(2)** ________________
Receptionist: **(3)** ________________
Phil: My name's Philip Jones.
Receptionist: OK. **(4)** ________________ ... Oh, Mr. Jones, I'm afraid he's on the other line. Would you like to hold?
Phil: Sure.
Bank clerk: Anthony Moore.
Phil: Hello. **(5)** ________________
Bank clerk: Oh, yes, Mr. Jones. Thank you for getting back to me so quickly. There seems to be a problem with your account.
Phil: Oh? What kind of problem?
Bank clerk: Well, you've overdrawn your account by more than $500. You really need to come to the bank to discuss it. **(6)** ________________
Phil: I'm busy today. Would tomorrow be convenient for you?
Bank clerk: Yes, that's fine. Ten thirty?
Phil: Yes, ten thirty's fine for me.
Bank clerk: Well, thank you for calling. **(7)** ________________
Phil: Goodbye.

2.43 **Listen and check.**

3 2.44 **Listen and repeat the expressions from Conversations A and B.**

4 Work with a partner. Choose one of the situations below and write a telephone conversation.

a Phil calls his friend Jeff and arranges to meet him this evening.
b Phil calls Smiths Insurance and arranges a meeting with Mrs. Bella Watson

Practice your conversation.

Life Skills: Creativity & Imagination
Brainstorming

1 2.45 **Listen to the notes about brainstorming. Have you ever used brainstorming to come up with new ideas?**

2 Work with a partner. In one minute, brainstorm all the English words you can about your cell phone. Write them under these headings:

features looks materials uses

3 Work in groups. You are the creative team in an advertising agency. Your client wants you to come up with an innovative approach to selling their new cell phone. Hold a brainstorming meeting. What ideas did you come up with?

MACMILLAN LIFE SKILLS

11 Vocabulary Extra

Idiomatic expressions

1 **Look at the dictionary extracts defining some fixed idiomatic expressions – sometimes known as "binomials." Replace the underlined phrases in the sentences (a-e) with a suitable binomial.**

a His English is coming along very quickly.
b There aren't many sandwiches left, so you won't be able to make a careful selection of what you want.
c It's all there in written form.
d Her clothes were lying scattered in several different places on the floor.
e We see each other sometimes, but not often.

Check your own dictionary. Which word do you need to look up to find the expression?

2 **There is one mistake in each of the underlined idiomatic expressions in the sentences (a-f). Look at the relevant dictionary extract and correct the mistake.**

a Di has a young family and runs her own business. She certainly has her fingers full.
b Hugo is hopeless with money. He's over his neck in debt.
c Petra sometimes makes mistakes, but her heart is in its right place.
d Sue is always wearing fantastic clothes. She has one eye for fashion.
e Tim's business isn't making much money, but he keeps his head above the water.
f Boris got a fantastic job straight after college. He really landed on his foot.

Do any of your family, friends, or colleagues fit these descriptions? Tell a partner about them.

3 **Use the words in the box to complete the idiomatic expressions (a-f) describing feelings and emotions.**

arms	dumps	minds	moon	stitches	weather

a to be in ______________
b to be of two ______________
c to be over the ______________
d to be up in ______________
e to be under the ______________
f to be down in the ______________

Check your ideas in the dictionary extracts. Think about the last time you felt any of these emotions. Ask your partner.

When was the last time you were over the moon?

PHRASE **in black and white** in a written or printed form

PHRASE **here and there** in or to several different places

PHRASE **by/in leaps and bounds** used for saying that something improves quickly or increases a lot

PHRASE **(every) now and then/again** sometimes, but not regularly or often

PHRASE **pick and choose (sth)** to choose the things you prefer, rather than simply accepting what you are given

PHRASE **sb's heart is in the right place** used for saying that someone tries to do good things even though it does not always seem like this

PHRASE **keep your head above water** *informal* to manage to live or keep a business working even though you are not earning much money

PHRASE **have your hands full** to be extremely busy

PHRASE **land on your feet** to be lucky and get into a good situation after being in a difficult one

PHRASE **have an eye for** to have a natural ability for seeing or noticing something

PHRASE **up to your neck in sth** *informal* involved or busy with something

PHRASE **up in arms** angry and complaining about something

PHRASE **(down) in the dumps** *informal* feeling unhappy

PHRASE **be of two minds (about sth)** to not be certain about something, or to have difficulty in making a decision

PHRASE **be over the moon (about sth)** *British informal* to be very happy about something

PHRASE **in stitches** *informal* laughing a lot

PHRASE **under the weather** *informal* not feeling well

From the *Macmillan Essential Dictionary for Learners of American English.*

4 **Check your own dictionary. Look up your six favorite idiomatic expressions on this page and answer the questions.**

a Which word do you look for first?
b How are the idiomatic expressions organized?
c What examples are given?

12 Style

READING

1 **Which of these statements are similar to your views? Talk about your sense of style with a partner.**

a I love modern fashion and I always keep up with the trends.
b People shouldn't care so much about their appearance.
c I like wearing unusual patterns and colors.
d I wear whatever is comfortable and I don't care what it looks like.
e I save up for designer brands.
f I often shop for handmade clothes.
g I like to stand out in a crowd.

2 **Read the article below. Which of the statements in Exercise 1 might be said by someone who likes vintage clothing?**

Vintage Style

For some people, the idea of searching through old clothes is really not appealing at all. For others, it is heaven. These people prefer to describe old clothes as *pre-loved*, *recycled*, or *vintage*. In these days of mass production and cheap fashion, some people look for clothes that have been tailored or sewn by hand. Lovers of vintage clothing say that the cut and fit of clothes from the 1940s and1950s is better than today's clothes. The clothes were made to last and not to be thrown away after one season's wear. Some of the most popular items are, for women, pretty dresses with floral patterns; silk blouses with covered buttons; skirts and jackets in good quality fabric; cashmere sweaters; and shapely 1940s swimwear. Men usually look for handmade jackets and coats; smart high-waisted trousers that can be worn with suspenders; collarless cotton shirts; and waistcoats. If you are curious about this style of clothing, you will find plenty of choice. Market stalls or charity shops are not the only places to look — you can also find a lot of interesting clothing online now. Check out the clothing bloggers who give useful advice on where to find interesting pieces and how to wear them.

3 **Underline the correct information according to the article.**

a Old clothes are sometimes described as **recycled** / **retired**.
b In earlier decades clothing was made to be **thrown away** / **worn** for a long time.
c **Trousers** / **dresses** can be worn with suspenders.
d If you want vintage clothing, there is **very little** / **plenty of** choice these days.
e Bloggers can offer **useless** / **useful** advice.

4 **Look at the two photographs. With a partner take it in turns to describe what the people are wearing.**

Think of a person you know who has an interesting sense of style. Describe them to your partner.

5 Pairwork **Student A:** page iii
Student B: page vi

- **Grammar:** Adjective order. *have something done.*
- **Vocabulary:** Clothes. Physical description. Verb phrases.
- **Language for Life:** Small talk

VOCABULARY & LISTENING

1 Look at the items of clothing and complete the descriptions below. Use your dictionary if necessary.

a fabulous Mexican snakeskin *cowboy boots*
b a stylish pinstriped ____________
c old baggy ____________
d a plain green cotton ____________
e a red low-waisted ____________
f a wide black leather ____________
g high red leather ____________
h old black skinny ____________
i a short-sleeved checked ____________
j a long-sleeved black and white striped ____________
k a beautiful long purple silk evening ____________
l a bright orange turtleneck ____________

1 
belt

2 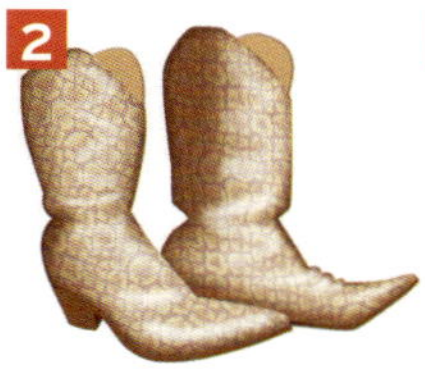
cowboy boots

3 
boots

4 
shirt

5 
dress

6 
miniskirt

7 
sweatshirt

8 
suit

9 
jeans

10 
sweater

11 
jeans

12 
top

2 2.46 **Listen to four people (Al, Fran, Jay, and Brooke) talking about clothes. Identify their favorite items from the list in Exercise 1. Which of the items of clothing in Exercise 1 do you like/dislike?**

1 
2 
3 
4 

GRAMMAR

1 Put the adjectives describing Al, Fran, Jay, and Brooke's favorite clothes in the correct columns.

Opinion	Size / Shape	Age	Pattern / Color	Origin	Material / Style	NOUN
1 *fabulous*				*Mexican*	*snakeskin*	*cowboy boots*

2 Put the adjectives in the right order to describe these clothes.

a a/an / linen / dark blue / elegant / jacket
an elegant dark blue linen jacket
b a / V-neck / black / brand-new / T-shirt
c a/an / silk / white / expensive / blouse
d a / beige / woolen / plain / sweater
e a/an / fur / old / Russian / hat
f blue / scruffy / suede / shoes

Use three adjectives to describe the most interesting item of clothing in your closet.

READING

1 Read the description of people waiting for a job interview. Are the following statements true or false?

- **a** All the other people in the waiting room are candidates.
- **b** One of the candidates is wealthy.
- **c** Three of the candidates are wearing white shirts.
- **d** The interviewer is younger than the candidates.

You are waiting for a job interview. Your first interview since leaving college. You are nervous. There are three other people in the waiting room. Your appointment is for 3pm. It is 2.30 and you wonder whether the other people will go in before or after you, and who will be successful.

Will it be the guy with a scar across the left eyebrow and sitting with his legs casually crossed? He is between 25 and 30 years old, just under six feet tall, average build, wearing a white, open-necked shirt and smart, grey pants. You notice he is wearing an expensive wristwatch. He has brown eyes and hair, and he also has a tan, probably just got back from vacation in the Caribbean. He is relaxed and confident, at least he appears to be.

Or will it be the woman with the preppy glasses, wearing a floral vintage dress and sensible sandals? She looks more mature than the other candidates, but that might just be her clothes. She is looking round at you and reading something from a file – she is clearly doing her preparation.

The third person is a younger woman, your sort of age, with blonde curly hair. She is wearing blue jeans with a white shirt and a smart navy blazer. It looks cool but maybe not right for an interview? She is biting her nails while staring at her cell phone.

Just then, the lady in the vintage dress stands up and introduces herself: she is the interviewer! She has been observing you for the last half hour. She invites you to follow her into the next office and the interview begins.

2 Complete these sentences with information about yourself.

- **a** I am ________________ years old.
- **b** I've got ________________, ________________ hair.
- **c** I would wear ________________ and ________________ for an interview.
- **d** I come over as ________________ in an interview.

3 Work with a partner. Discuss the questions.

- **a** What kinds of things do you notice about a person when you meet them for the first time?
- **b** What can you tell about a person from a first meeting?
- **c** Are your first impressions of people usually right?

PRONUNCIATION

1 Look at these words with different vowel combinations. Link the words with the same vowel sounds.

a	/i/	medium	bald	author
b	/u/	plain	beige	fur
c	/ɜr/	tall	blue	hair
d	/ɔ/	third	green	jeans
e	/eɪ/	two	their	suede
f	/er/	wear	worse	suits

2 2.47 **Listen, check, and repeat.**

VOCABULARY & WRITING

1 **Complete the information about the man in the description on page 110.**

Age: *between 25 and 30*	Height: ______	Build: ______
Eyes: ______	Hair: ______	Distinguishing features: ______

2 **Match the words and phrases in the box to the categories in Exercise 1. Use your dictionary if necessary and find at least one other suitable word for each category.**

bald blond streaks deep-set freckles a goatee hazel in her early thirties in her mid-twenties in his late teens just over 1 meter 80 medium messy a mole overweight receding red sideburns shoulder-length slim stocky a tattoo well-built

3 **Read descriptions (a–c) of different roles the movie star Johnny Depp has played. Match the descriptions to the movies.**

a He has a mustache and a goatee and messy black shoulder-length hair. His eyes are dark brown and he wears black eyeliner. He has a tattoo on one of his arms.

b He's tall and skinny with large deep-set eyes and a sad expression on his thin face. His hair is messy, and there are scars on his cheeks.

c He has wavy black hair with a gray streak in the front and long bushy sideburns. He has dark shadows under his eyes and lines on his forehead.

1 Edward Scissorhands

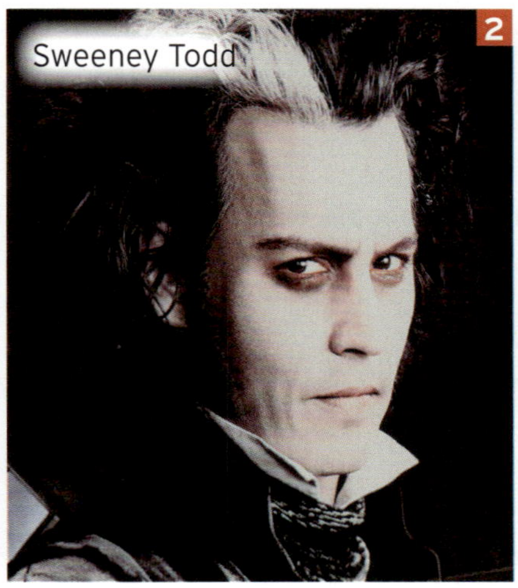
2 Sweeney Todd

3 Pirates of the Caribbean

Now match each of the movies to the year of its release: 1990, 2003, 2007.

4 **Write a description of a movie character. Read it aloud. Your partner guesses who it is.**

SPEAKING: ANECDOTE

1 2.48 **Listen to Martin talking about a person he met for the first time recently. Put a cross (✗) by the answers that are wrong.**

a Where were you when you met this person? **At a friend's engagement party.**
b Was the person a man or a woman? **It was a woman.**
c Who introduced you? **She introduced herself.**
d What was your first impression? **I thought she was funny and very confident.**
e What did she look like? **She was tall with long curly black hair.**
f Did you notice anything special about her? **She was wearing a turquoise ring.**
g What did you talk about? **We talked about Mexico.**
h Did you find anything in common? **We'd both been to the same place on vacation.**
i Have you seen the person again? **Yes, I have.**

Correct the wrong answers. Listen again if necessary.

2 **You are going to tell your partner about somebody you met for the first time recently.**

- Ask yourself the questions in Exercise 1.
- Think about *what* to say and *how* to say it.
- Tell your partner about the person.

LISTENING

1 **Look at the pictures of Tony Goodwin and Marilyn Cook who took part in a TV show called *Ten Years Younger*. Discuss these questions with a partner.**

a How old do you think Tony and Marilyn are?
b What differences can you see between the *Before* and *After* pictures?

2 2.49 **Listen to two friends, Annie and Betty, discussing the TV show and check whether your ideas in Exercise 1 were right.**

3 **Make sentences with these words and phrases to describe what Tony and Marilyn had done.**

Tony had his Marilyn had her	clothes eyelids hair make-up teeth	cut and colored. chosen by a stylist. done by an expert. lifted. whitened.

Listen again and check. Do you know people who look young for their age? Tell your partner about them.

GRAMMAR

have *something* done

She's **had** her hair **cut**.

She **hasn't had** it **colored**.

Has she **had** it **styled**?
Yes, she has.
No, she hasn't.

1 **Work with your partner. In each of these sentences, who cut Tony's hair?**

a Tony cut his hair.
b Tony had his hair cut.

2 **Work with your partner. Complete the table below with the correct verb forms.**

	Do it yourself	Have it done
a	I like washing my hair.	I like **(1)** ___*having*___ my hair washed.
b	I never color my hair.	I never **(2)** ____________ colored.
c	I'm cutting my hair next week.	I **(3)** ____________ next week.
d	I **(4)** ____________ last month.	I had my teeth cleaned last month.
e	I pierced my ears.	**(5)** ____________ .
f	**(6)** ____________ .	I want to have my bathroom repainted.

Cross out unlikely or unusual sentences. Check (✓) any sentences that are true for you.

3 **Have it done or do it yourself? Complete the questions as in the example.**

a If your car was dirty, would you (wash) ____________ ?
... would you have it washed or would you wash it yourself?
b If your winter coat was dirty, would you (clean) ____________ ?
c If your bicycle had a flat tire, would you (repair) ____________ ?
d If your house needed redecorating, would you (do) ____________ ?
e If your kitchen knives were blunt, would you (sharpen) ____________ ?
f If your new pants were too long, would you (hem) ____________ ?

Work with your partner. Ask and answer the questions.

4 **Grammar Extra 12** page xvii. Read the explanation and do the exercises.

VOCABULARY & SPEAKING

1 **Match the verbs in box A with the noun phrases in box B to describe the kinds of things people do before they leave the house in the morning.**

A	
do	get
have	make
put	read
take	turn

B

the bed · breakfast · the children ready · some coffee · the computer on · a cup of tea · the dishes · dressed · my email · my exercises · my homework · my make-up on · the newspaper · the radio on · a shower · the TV on

2 **Getting dressed is one of the routine things we must do every morning. Think about how you go about getting dressed quickly.**

a How do you decide what you are going to wear? Do you plan the night before what clothes you will wear?

b Do you try on several outfits before making a decision?

c How often do you make the wrong choice in clothes?

Compare with a partner. What are the differences?

READING & VOCABULARY

1 **Read through these two descriptions. Underline the correct alternatives.**

How I Shop for Clothes

Person A: I really enjoy shopping for clothes. I do it in a very organized way. Twice a year I go **(1) <u>through</u>** / **out of** my wardrobe and get rid of all the things I haven't **(2) worn** / **seen** in the past six months. Then I do some research into the latest "looks" for the next season and make a list of all the things I need. I then head out to my favorite stores. I go to the same place for my basic wardrobe items like pants, jackets, and shirts, because I know that the quality is good and the cut **(3) matches** / **suits** me. I usually buy a complete outfit so that I don't get home with, say, a great new jacket and find I have nothing that **(4) goes** / **wears** with it. When I need an outfit for a special occasion I go to a lovely place called Xtra Style. There they stock fabulous designer items and I can **(5) try on** / **take off** as many things as I like and the assistants always have plenty of time to help me find the right thing.

Person B: I like to be well-dressed, but I do not like **(6) trying on** / **going to** clothes shops. As soon as I get into a store I get really confused by all the choice and immediately just want to go **(7) in** / **home** again! I often come home with nothing. So, these days I buy all my clothes online. It's fantastic! I can **(8) sit** / **get** down with a cup of coffee and spend as long as I like browsing my favorite stores. I order items in different sizes and colors and try them **(9) on** / **off** in the comfort of my own home. I love getting my purchases delivered to my door, it always feels exciting to open **(10) up** / **out** the packages. If I need a second opinion about how something **(11) looks** / **wears** on me, I can ask my daughter. She is always honest about what **(12) suits** / **matches** me. The only downside is having to send **(13) back** / **away** the items that I don't want, but that's still better than the torture of a shopping trip ...

▶ 2.50 **Do you think these are descriptions of a man or a woman? Listen and check.**

2 **Complete the questions with the verbs in the box.**

fit · get dressed · look good on · match · try on · wear

a What colors ______________ you?

b How long does it take you to ______________ ?

c Do you like to ______________ lots of different clothes in stores?

d Do you usually ______________ a watch?

e Do your brother or sister's clothes ______________ you?

f Do you try to wear tops that ______________ your eye color?

Work with your partner. Ask and answer the questions.

3 **Work with your partner. How would you get ready for some of these occasions?**

- a job interview
- a wedding
- a first date
- a long flight
- an evening at the theater
- a Saturday night out with your friends
- a day at the beach
- a Sunday afternoon walk around town

A job interview: I'd take a shower. I'd put on a clean shirt and a suit. I'd ...

LANGUAGE FOR LIFE

1 **Work with a partner. Which of the things in the box do you think people are most likely to talk about at a wedding?**

a politics b the weather c the bride and groom d each other's clothes
e world peace f the enjoyable occasion g current divorce rates h the food

2 2.51 **Read and listen to five conversations at a wedding. Match each conversation with a topic from Exercise 1.**

1

A: Oh, she looks so beautiful.
B: She does, doesn't she? He's a lucky, lucky man.
A: He is.

2

C: What a beautiful day!
D: It is. So sunny. And really warm for this time of year.
C: I know. I don't think I need my jacket.

3

E: What a beautiful dress.
F: Oh, this? I've had it for ages.
E: Well, blue really looks good on you. It brings out the color of your eyes.
F: Do you think so? Thank you. And that's a very nice hat.
E: Oh, I'm glad you like it. I got it on sale – it was a bargain.
F: Was it? Well, it looks like a million dollars.

4

G: This dessert is delicious.
H: It is, isn't it?
G: Don't you want your strawberry?
H: Yes, I do. I was just saving it. Don't take it!

5

I: Thank you so much for a wonderful day. We've had a great time.
J: You're welcome. I'm glad you could make it.
I: Oh, we wouldn't have missed it for the world. Right, Arthur?
K: Mm? Oh, no, we wouldn't. Absolutely. Thank you for inviting us.
J: Oh, don't mention it. Well, have a safe trip home.
I: We will. Goodbye.

3 **Complete the sentences with the useful phrases from the conversations in Exercise 2.**

Making positive comments

a "Oh, she looks so beautiful."
b "________________ day!"
c "This dessert ________________ ."

Giving and receiving compliments

d "What a beautiful dress!" "Oh this? I've had it for ages."
e "Blue ________________." "________________ think so? Thank you."
f "________________ nice hat." "I'm ________________ ."

Thanking and accepting thanks

g "Thank you so much for a wonderful day." "You're welcome."
h "________________ inviting us." "Don't ________________."

2.52 **Listen, check, and repeat.**

4 **Work with your partner. Write a conversation between two people at a wedding.**

Choose from the following options.

- the bride's mother and the groom's mother
- the bride's grandmother and a bridesmaid
- the groom and his best man

Practice your conversation.

Life Skills: Influencing
Shopping

1 **Work with a partner. Think about what influences your decisions when you go shopping. Select the top three from the list below.**

Word of mouth
Press reviews
Internet bloggers
TV advertising
Celebrity endorsements
Friend recommendation

2 **Choose an item of clothing or an accessory you own, and make notes on how you could persuade someone to buy it.**

Word of mouth (e.g. *I heard it was popular ...*)
Internet blogger (e.g. *MyFashDiary calls it one of the ...*)
TV advertising (e.g. *The ad features a famous model ...*)
Celebrity endorsements (e.g. *Alexa Chung was seen wearing ...*)
Friend recommendations (e.g. *Sarah think it's ...*)

3 **Now try to influence your partner to buy an item of clothing. Use your notes from Exercise 2 to persuade your partner to buy the item.**

MACMILLAN LIFE SKILLS

12 Vocabulary Extra

Exploring meanings

1 Work with a partner. Look at the dictionary extract for *suspect* and discuss the questions.

a How many dictionary entries are there for the word *suspect*?
b Is *suspect* more commonly used as a noun, a verb, or an adjective?
c What is the difference in pronunciation between *suspect* as a verb, and *suspect* as a noun or adjective?
d How many meanings are explained for the verb *suspect*?
e Which is the most common meaning of the verb *suspect*?

2 Look at the sentences (a–e). Identify the correct dictionary entry and the correct meaning of *suspect*.

a Do you really **suspect** him of taking your money? = entry 1 (verb), meaning 2
b Dave is a **suspect** in the case of the missing money.
c The officer **suspected** that Burns had been involved all along.
d A **suspect** object has been disposed of at JFK airport.
e His motives were **suspect**. He seemed too good to be true.

3 Homographs are words that are spelled the same but have a different meaning and sometimes a different pronunciation. Match the example sentences with the correct pronunciation.
Use the dictionary extracts to help you.

1
a Just a **minute**, I'm on the phone. — 1 /maɪˈnut/
b The cake she gave me was **minute**! — 2 /ˈmɪnɪt/

2
a Do you shake hands in China, or **bow**? — 1 /baʊ/
b I love that pink **bow** in her hair. — 2 /boʊ/

3
a I've seen The Killers **live** in concert twice. — 1 /lɪv/
b Where do you **live**? — 2 /laɪv/

Use your own dictionary and look up the different meanings and pronunciation for six more homographs in the box.

close lead perfect row tear refuse

4 Look at the dictionary entry for the adjective *soft*. It shows seven different meanings.
Match the sentences (a–g) with the meanings (1–7).

a I love the **soft** purring noise of a sleeping cat.
b People who seem scary are actually often really **soft**.
c Pasta should be eaten "al dente" – not overcooked and **soft**!
d In a bedroom, **soft** pastel shades are better than bright, primary colors.
e It's better to wash your clothes in **soft** water rather than hard water.
f Cashmere is a **soft** material. In fact it's the softest material for clothes.
g Most parents are too **soft** with their children. Bring back discipline!

Which of the above statements do you agree with? Discuss with your partner.

Check your own dictionary. How does it show the information for words that belong to more than one word class and/or have more than one meaning?

---

bow[1] /baʊ/ verb **1** [I] to bend your body forward from the waist in order to show respect for someone **2** [I/T] to bend your head

bow[3] /boʊ/ noun [C] **1** a weapon made from a curved piece of wood. It is used for shooting ARROWS. **2** a knot that has two circular parts and two loose ends: *The ribbon was tied in a bow.* **3** an object that you use for playing instruments such as the VIOLIN

live[1] /lɪv/ verb ★★★
1 [I] to be alive, or to stay alive: *Aunt Joan **lived to be** 86.* ♦ *Hippodamus **lived in** the early fifth century B.C.* ♦ **live to do sth** (=live long enough to do it) *He lived to see the first talking pictures.*
2 [I] to have your home in a particular place: *Paris is a nice place to live.* ♦ *They **lived in** a studio apartment in Manhattan.*

live[3] /laɪv/ adv **1** if something is broadcast live, it is happening at the same time as you are watching it or listening to it **2** if something is performed live, it is performed in front of an audience

min•ute /ˈmɪnɪt/ noun [C] ★★★
1 a period of 60 seconds. There are 60 minutes in one hour: *I'll meet you downstairs in ten minutes.* ♦ *A bus leaves at five minutes after the hour.*

mi•nute /maɪˈnut/ adj **1** very small: *The soil contained minute quantities of uranium.*
2 very careful and detailed: *a minute examination of the evidence*

soft /sɔft/ adj ★★★

1 not hard/firm	5 not strict enough
2 not rough/stiff	6 kind/sympathetic
3 quiet/nice	7 about water
4 pale/gentle	

1 a soft substance is easy to press or shape and is not hard or firm: *soft cheese* ♦ *The soil is fairly soft after the rain.*
2 a soft material or surface is nice to touch and not rough or stiff: *I want to get a nice soft carpet for the bedroom.* ♦ *Her skin **felt soft** to his touch.*
3 a soft sound is quiet and nice to listen to: *The engine noise was no more than a soft hum.*
4 a soft light or color is pale, gentle, and nice to look at: *Her bedroom was decorated in soft shades of pink and blue.*
5 not strict enough with other people and allowing them to do things they should not do: *You're **too soft** – I wouldn't let them behave like that.* ♦ *They accused the governor of being **soft on** crime.*
6 kind and sympathetic: *He must have **a soft heart** beneath that stern exterior.*
7 soft water does not contain many MINERALS (=natural substances) and is easy to use with soap

sus•pect[1] /səˈspekt/ verb [T] ★★
1 to believe that something is true: **+(that)** *Police suspected that she had some connection with the robbery.*
2 to think that someone might have done something bad: *He wrote a letter naming the people whom he suspected.* ♦ **suspect sb of sth** *men suspected of involvement in the bombing*
3 to think that something might be bad: *Carl seemed very kind, but she suspected his motives.*

Word family: suspect
Words in the same family as ***suspect***
- **suspected** *adj*
- **suspicious** *adj*
- **unsuspecting** *adj*
- **suspicion** *n*
- **suspiciously** *adv*

sus•pect[2] /ˈsʌˌspekt/ noun [C] **1** someone who might have committed a crime: *a murder suspect* **2** something that might have caused something bad

sus•pect[3] /ˈsʌˌspekt/ adj **1** something that is suspect might not be good, honest, or reliable: *suspect motives* **2** a suspect object might be dangerous or illegal: *a suspect package*

From the *Macmillan Essential Dictionary for Learners of American English.*

Review D

GRAMMAR

Grammar Extra pages xiii-xvii.

1 Cross out *who/which/that* when it can be left out.

a *India* is the country ~~which~~ I'd most like to visit.
b There are only a few *sports* **that** really interest me.
c I still have the first *CD* **that** I ever bought.
d I don't like people **who** *don't tell the truth.*
e The person **who** I spend most time with is *my friend Ben*.

Change the words in italics to make true sentences. Compare with a partner.

2 Complete each sentence so that it means the same as the sentence before it.

a If you don't wear a jacket, you'll catch a cold. = Unless you *wear a jacket, you'll catch a cold.*
b We'll have to go unless they arrive in the next five minutes. = If they ______
c If they don't work, they'll fail the exam. = Unless they ______
d He won't come to the party unless you ask him. = If you ______
e You won't be able to buy that car if you don't save your money. = Unless you ______

3 Write the words in the correct order to make questions. Change to contracted forms where possible.

a know / you / what / doing / Do / are / next weekend / you ?
Do you know what you're doing next weekend?
b you / Can / you / your shoes / me / bought / tell / where ?
c think / you / politics / interesting / topic / is / an / Do ?
d you / born / me / you / where / were / Could / tell ?

Work with your partner. Ask and answer the questions.

4 Complete the unreal conditional sentences.

a If I (be) *were you*, I (drive) *'d drive* more carefully.
b If I (study) ______ harder for yesterday's exam, I (pass) ______ .
c We (learn) ______ a lot from animals if they (can) ______ talk.
d If I (not fall) ______ asleep, I (see) ______ the rest of the movie.
e I (can) ______ call Cleo now if I (have) ______ my cell phone.
f I (not buy) ______ this car if I (know) ______ it was so unreliable.

5 Underline the correct alternative.

a I wish I **could have done** / **can do** more with my life.
b If only I **am** / **was** more interested in money.
c I wish I **were** / **had been** ten years younger.
d If only I **didn't start** / **hadn't started** smoking.
e I wish I **have** / **had** more free time.
f If only I **was** / **had been** born in the USA.

Which statements are true for you? Discuss with your partner.

6 Look at the pictures and underline the correct verb forms.

a

b

c

d

a He **had his hair cut** / **cut his hair**.
b He **had his hair cut** / **cut his hair**.
c She's **fixing her car** / **having her car fixed**.
d She's **fixing her car** / **having her car fixed**.

VOCABULARY

1 Complete the story with the words in the box.

about me   at me   me in   me off   me up   ~~of me~~

Sadly, my mom and dad died when I was very young, and I went to live with my grandparents. They took care **(1)** ___of me___ and I always felt really loved. At night, my grandma always used to tuck **(2)** ________ . When I was older, if I stayed out late, they would worry **(3)** ________ , and then, when I got home, they would tell **(4)** ________ but they never yelled **(5)** ________ . I think they brought **(6)** ________ well and made me the man I am today.

2 Complete the text with the correct form of *make* or *let*.

I went to boarding school. The teachers were really nice. They **(1)** ___let___ us wear any style of clothing we wanted and they **(2)** ________ us use their first names, too. Of course, there were still rules. They **(3)** ________ us keep our rooms neat and they **(4)** ________ us do our homework every evening. Overall, though, I would say they were very liberal. They even **(5)** ________ one girl color her hair pink!

3 Complete the sentences with the adverbs.

~~Apparently~~   Basically   definitely   Hopefully   incredibly   very much   very well

a ___Apparently___ , Jane is having an affair with Tom.
b Fay is ________ smart. She knows everything!
c Ruth can play the saxophone ________ .
d ________ , I'll pass my exams and get a good job.
e I'm ________ going out tonight. I need some fun!
f I don't really enjoy academic work ________ .
g ________ , I think I'm fantastic!

4 Put the words in the box in the correct group (a–c).

~~baggy~~   ~~blouse~~   boots   checked   ~~cotton~~   leather   linen   long-sleeved
plain   silk   striped   suede   suit   sweater   top

a **material**: *cotton, ...*   b **shape/design/pattern**: *baggy, ...*   c **clothes**: *blouse, ...*

PRONUNCIATION

1 Look at some words from Units 10–12. Say the words and add them to the table.

~~adventurous~~   apparently   ~~audition~~   ~~awful~~   Christmas   develop   ~~dinosaur~~   elegant
exercise   expensive   language   pajamas   psychiatrist   ridiculous   talented   vintage

A: ■■■ (Ooo)	*dinosaur*
B: ■■ (Oo)	*awful*
C: ■■■ (oOo)	*audition*
D: ■■■■ (oOoo)	*adventurous*

2 Underline the stressed syllable in each word.

2.53 **Listen, check, and repeat.**

READING & LISTENING

1 Online magazine *Blogspot* invited people to describe their lives in about 100 words. Read these three entries. Complete the sentences with the correct name.

a ________________ will miss her dog.
b ________________ enjoys sailing.
c ________________ was laid off.

blogspot.com

Blogspot

HOME ABOUT BLOG CONTACT search

Gill – I work as a teacher in a high school. I teach Chemistry, Biology, and Physics. I love my job even though it's very tiring and not well paid. I think I'm happier now than I was 20 years ago, when I was in my teens. I used to worry all the time about how I looked and whether I would ever find a boyfriend! I think I'll be even happier when I can retire and do all the things I enjoy, like hiking and sailing. I just hope I stay fit and healthy enough to have a long and active retirement.

David – I have been having a difficult time recently. Unfortunately, I was laid off six months ago and I haven't managed to find another job. It's not that easy when you're in your fifties. Just recently I decided that I need to approach the problem in a different way. I am going to train to be a self-employed driving instructor. That way I will be my own boss and no one can fire me! It has been a very tough year for me and my wife, but I know things are going to get better. I am optimistic about the future.

Carrie – I'm going to college in the fall and I am really excited. I will be studying Engineering and hope to work in the auto industry when I graduate. I have always loved cars. When I was three, my parents bought me a cute little red pedal car and they say that I loved it so much I ate my meals in it! My best friend, Zara, is going to the same college, so we are going to be roommates. I'm looking forward to moving away from home and becoming more independent, but I'll miss my dog ... and my parents!

2 Read the texts again. Are these sentences true or false?

a Gill has happy memories of her teenage years.
b David is married.
c Carrie has a best friend called Clare.
d David has had an easy time recently.
e Gill is looking forward to her retirement.
f Carrie doesn't want to leave home.

3 2.54 **Listen to retired businessman Colin talking about his life. What does he regret about his past?**

4 Listen again and number the events of Colin's life in order, 1-7.

1 *e*, 2 ...

a He got married.
b He worked in a factory.
c He became a cab driver.
d He started his own business.
e He went to live with Ida and Bud.
f He played by the railroad tracks.
g He had two children.

WRITING & SPEAKING

1 Read Karen's email to an old school friend. Complete the text with the linking words in the box.

After although and ~~but~~ so unfortunately When While who

mail.com

Compose
Inbox
Drafts
Sent
Spam
Trash

To: anitamanning@heatmail.com
Cc:
Subject:
From: kwilson@madisonhigh.org

Dear Anita,

It was great to get your email through schoolfriends.com. How many years is it since we last saw each other? I don't want to think about it!

A Life's had its ups and downs, **(1)** ___but___ generally things have turned out OK for me.

B **(2)** __________ high school, I went to college in Baltimore, and studied drama. **(3)** __________ I graduated, I got a job with a small theater group which worked with children in schools all over the country. I traveled a lot, and loved it.

C **(4)** __________ I was working at a school in Detroit, I met and married Mike, **(5)** __________ was an English teacher. I left my job, and we had two children, Perry and Dylan, who are now 13 and 15. But **(6)** __________, Mike and I split up six years ago. Perry and Dylan live with me now, and **(7)** __________ we are divorced, Mike and I have stayed friends.

D I didn't have a lot of money as a single parent, and life was tough for a while. But a few years ago I wanted to start working again, **(8)** __________ I retrained as a drama teacher. I love my job **(9)** __________ guess where I'm working now? That's right, Madison High, our old school!

E I'm getting married in June to a man named Felipe. He's retiring in a few years, and we're planning to go traveling in Europe and Asia when the boys move out. It would be great to meet up sometime. I wish I'd kept in touch with more friends from high school. Do you ever see Michelle or Rachel? I'd love to know what they're doing now.

Best regards,
Karen

2 Match the questions (1-5) to the paragraphs (A-E) in the email.

1 What has happened in your personal life? *C*
2 What has happened in your school or professional life?
3 What are your hopes for the future?
4 How has your life been up to now?
5 What are you doing now?

3 Think about your own answers to the questions in Exercise 2. Make notes.

4 Tell your partner about your life up to now, what you're doing now, and your hopes for the future. Use the notes you made in Exercise 3.

After I graduated from high school, I moved to Chile to live with my dad. We were living in Santiago. One evening I ...

5 Write an email to an old childhood friend about your life up to now, what you're doing now, and your hopes for the future.

Pairwork: Student A

UNIT 7: Experiences

What experiences has Student B had?

- Write Student B's name in the space below.
- Write statements using phrases a-e that you think are true.
- Write questions to check your statements.
- Ask Student B the questions.

I think ______ (Student B's name) ...	Question	✓ = I'm more or less right. ✗ = I'm completely wrong.
a be burglarized *Isa has never been burglarized.*	*Have you ever been burglarized?*	______
b be stopped and searched by customs	______	______
c be let down by a friend	______	______
d be mistaken for somebody else	______	______
e be asked to make a speech	______	______

UNIT 8: Automatic pilot

You are going to complete a text with Student B's help.

- Student B has the same text as you but with different verbs missing.
- Complete the text with the most appropriate forms of the verbs in parentheses.
- Then take turns reading out your completed text and check your answers.

Two pilots (**1 fly**) *were flying* a passenger airline from Dallas to Mexico City, when one of the pilots **came out** of the cockpit to make some coffee. He (**3 have**) ______ problems with the coffee machine, so he **asked** his co-pilot to help him. As the co-pilot (**5 leave**) ______ the cockpit, he accidentally **closed** the door behind him and then immediately (**7 realize**) ______ that he'**d locked** them both out of the cockpit. The door (**9 be**) ______ fitted with an anti-terrorist lock which **was** impossible to open – even for the pilots. Fortunately, one of the pilots (**11 put**) ______ his Swiss army knife in his hand baggage which he **had stored** in a locker above one of the passenger seats. When he finally (**13 locate**) ______ the knife, the two pilots **managed** to break the lock. By the time the pilots (**15 break**) ______ into the cockpit, the plane **was cruising** eastwards over the Caribbean Sea.

UNIT 9: A funny story

You are going to complete a funny story with Student B's help. You have parts of the story already completed, and Student B has other parts.

- Dictate alternate lines of the story to Student B, and write down the sentences that Student B dictates to you.
- Compare your completed stories, which should be identical.

A woman was playing golf when she hit the ball into the woods. She went to look for it and found a frog in a trap.

a The frog asked her if she could release him from the trap.

b ________________

c So the woman freed the frog. Then the frog admitted that there was something he hadn't told her.

d ________________

e The woman replied that that was fine.

f ________________

g The frog warned her that her husband would be the most handsome man in the world and all the women would chase him.

h ________________

i The woman said that for her second wish she wanted to be the richest woman in the world.

j ________________

k The woman insisted that she didn't mind.

l ________________

m The woman replied that she wanted to have a mild heart attack.

UNIT 10: Call my bluff

You are going to read out three definitions of some common English words. The definitions with crosses (✗) are false, and the one with a check (✓) is true. Student B has to guess which definition (1, 2, or 3) is the correct one.

- Complete one false definition for each word. Use your imagination!
- Read out your definitions and see if Student B can guess which ones are correct.
- Then listen to Student B's definitions and guess which ones are correct.

a A "wimp" is ...
  1 a person who ________________ . ✗
  2 a person who is helpful and sympathetic. ✗
  3 a person who isn't brave. ✓

b A "clog" is ...
  1 a shoe that has a wooden sole. ✓
  2 an animal that ________________ . ✗
  3 a person who is not very smart. ✗

c A "doodle" is ...
  1 a picture you draw when you're bored or thinking about other things. ✓
  2 a small dog with curly hair. ✗
  3 something that ________________ . ✗

d A "jingle" is ...
  1 a place where ________________ . ✗
  2 an illness that is most common in children. ✗
  3 a short piece of music that is used in advertisements. ✓

UNIT 11: Dilemmas

You are going to guess what Student B would do in different situations.

- Read the dilemmas below, and guess whether Student B would answer 1, 2, or 3 in each case.
- Ask Student B questions to find out whether you guessed correctly.

a If you were in a subway and someone were listening to loud music from a boombox, what would you do?
  1 I'd go over and ask him/her to turn it off.
  2 I'd just look at him/her angrily.
  3 I'd do nothing – it's up to the management to enforce the rules.

b If you needed to borrow a small sum of money, who would you ask?
  1 I'd ask my parents.
  2 I'd ask a friend.
  3 I'd ask the bank.

c If you wanted some advice about your career, who would you ask?
  1 I'd ask my parents.
  2 I'd ask my teacher.
  3 I'd ask people on social media.

d If you wanted someone to help you choose an outfit for a special occasion, who would you ask?
  1 I'd ask my mother.
  2 I'd ask a friend.
  3 I wouldn't ask anybody – I'd prefer to go shopping on my own.

UNIT 12: Find the differences

Student B has a similar picture to yours.

- Do not show your picture to Student B.
- Ask and answer questions to find the differences between your picture and Student B's picture.
- How many differences can you find?

In your picture, is the man wearing a blue T-shirt?

No, he's wearing a gray T-shirt.

Pairwork: Student B

UNIT 7: Experiences

What experiences has Student A had?

- Write Student A's name in the space below.
- Write statements using phrases a-e that you think are true.
- Write questions to check your statements.
- Ask Student A the questions.

I think ________ (Student A's name) ...	Question	✓ = I'm more or less right. ✗ = I'm completely wrong.
a be injured playing sports *Karl has been injured playing sports.*	*Have you ever been injured playing sports?*	______
b be bitten by a snake	______________	______
c be given a gift they didn't like	______________	______
d be invited to a costume party	______________	______
e be interviewed on radio or TV	______________	______

UNIT 8: Automatic pilot

You are going to complete a text with Student A's help.

- Student A has the same text as you but with different verbs missing.
- Complete the text with the most appropriate forms of the verbs in parentheses.
- Then take turns reading out your completed text and check your answers.

Two pilots **were flying** a passenger airline from Dallas to Mexico City, when one of the pilots (**2 come out**) ___*came out*___ of the cockpit to make some coffee. He **was having** problems with the coffee machine, so he (**4 ask**) ______________ his co-pilot to help him. As the co-pilot **was leaving** the cockpit, he accidentally (**6 close**) ______________ the door behind him and then immediately **realized**
that he (**8 lock**) ______________ them both out of the cockpit. The door **had been** fitted with an anti-terrorist lock which (**10 be**) ______________ impossible to open – even for the pilots. Fortunately, one of the pilots **had put** his Swiss army knife in his hand baggage which he (**12 store**) ______________ in a locker above one of the passenger seats. When he finally **located** the knife, the two pilots (**14 manage**) ______________ to break the lock. By the time the pilots **had broken** into the cockpit, the plane (**16 cruise**) ______________ eastwards over the Caribbean Sea.

UNIT 9: A funny story

You are going to complete a funny story with Student A's help. You have parts of the story already completed, and Student A has other parts.

- Dictate alternate lines of the story to Student A, and write down the sentences that Student A dictates to you.
- Compare your completed stories, which should be identical.

A woman was playing golf when she hit the ball into the woods. She went to look for it and found a frog in a trap.

a ________________
b The frog told her that he would grant her three wishes.
c ________________
d He explained that she could have three wishes, but whatever she wished for, her husband would have ten times more.
e ________________
f The woman said that for her first wish she wanted to be the most beautiful woman in the world.
g ________________
h The woman insisted that that was fine, because she would be the most beautiful woman in the world, and he would only have eyes for her.
i ________________
j The frog warned her that her husband would be ten times richer than her.
k ________________
l The frog then asked her what she wanted her third wish to be.
m ________________

UNIT 10: Call my bluff

You are going to read out three definitions of some common English words. The definitions with crosses (✗) are false, and the one with a check (✓) is true. Student A has to guess which definition (1, 2, or 3) is the correct one.

- Complete one false definition for each word. Use your imagination!
- Read out your definitions and see if Student A can guess which ones are correct.
- Then listen to Student A's definitions and guess which ones are correct.

a A "bargain" is ...
1. something you buy that costs much less than normal. ✓
2. something you take when you have a headache. ✗
3. something you ________________ . ✗

b A "doozy" is ...
1. something that is extremely unusual or special. ✓
2. a place where ________________ . ✗
3. a person who isn't very attractive. ✗

c A "plug" is ...
1. a round piece of plastic that blocks a hole. ✓
2. something that ________________ . ✗
3. a small carpet that you put in front of a door. ✗

d A "stickleback" is ...
1. a type of glue used to stick things back together. ✗
2. a small river fish that has spikes along its back. ✓
3. a gadget that you use to ________________ . ✗

UNIT 11: Dilemmas

You are going to guess what Student A would do in different situations.

- Read the dilemmas below, and guess whether Student A would answer 1, 2, or 3 in each case.
- Ask Student A questions to find out whether you guessed correctly.

a If you won two tickets to go on vacation to New York for a week, who would you take?
  1 I'd take a friend.
  2 I'd take my boyfriend/girlfriend.
  3 I'd take a member of my family.

b If you saw your favorite actor in a restaurant, what would you do?
  1 I'd stare at him/her from a distance.
  2 I'd go up and ask for his/her autograph.
  3 I'd pretend I hadn't seen him/her.

c If you wanted to impress someone at a party, would you tell a few white lies about yourself?
  1 Never.
  2 Maybe.
  3 Definitely.

d If a lazy friend wanted to copy your homework, what would you do?
  1 I'd say yes.
  2 I'd say no.
  3 I'd say yes, but I'd ask them for a favor in return.

UNIT 12: Find the differences

Student A has a similar picture to yours.

- Do not show your picture to Student A.
- Ask and answer questions to find the differences between your picture and Student A's picture.
- How many differences can you find?

Grammar Extra

UNIT 7: Passive

Passive = *be* (*am*, *was*, *have been*, etc.) + past participle (*used*, *built*, etc.)

TENSES		ASPECT			MODALS *will (would)*
		Simple	Progressive	Perfect	
Present	+	It's **used**.	It**'s being used**.	It **has been used**.	It **will be used**.
	-	It **isn't used**.	It **isn't being used**.	It **hasn't been used**.	It **won't be used**.
	?	**Is** it **used**?	**Is** it **being used**?	**Has** it **been used**?	**Will** it **be used**?
Past	+	It **was used**.	It **was being used**.	It **had been used**.	
	-	It **wasn't used**.	It **wasn't being used**.	It **hadn't been used**.	
	?	**Was** it **used**?	**Was** it **being used**?	**Had** it **been used**?	

The progressive forms *be being* and *been being* are very rare. Avoid using them.

In passive sentences, the object of the active verb becomes the subject of the passive verb. In other words, the "receiver" of the action becomes the subject and comes at the beginning of the sentence.

Active	Passive
subject verb object Somebody's stolen **my purse**!	subject verb **My purse** has been stolen!
subject verb object Detectives have arrested **two men**.	subject verb **Two men** have been arrested.
subject verb object President Roosevelt opened **the Golden Gate Bridge**.	subject verb by + agent **The Golden Gate Bridge** was opened by President Roosevelt.

In passive sentences, the "doer" of the action – known as the "agent" – is either not mentioned at all, or mentioned at the end of the sentence in a *by*-phrase.

There are several reasons why you might want to use passive verb structures.

1 The "doer" of the action is unknown.
Their house ***was built*** *in the 1980s.* (They don't know who built it.)

2 The "doer" of the action is not important in the context.
"When ***was*** *the Sydney Opera House* ***built****?" "In 1957."* (I want to know when it was ***built*** not who built it.)

3 The "doer" of the action is obvious.
Demonstrators ***were arrested*** *and* ***charged*** *with disturbing the peace.* (It is obvious that the police arrested and charged them.)

4 The "receiver" of the action is what we are talking about, and the "doer" is the new information. Generally, you tend to put "known" information at the beginning of a sentence and "new" information at the end. Compare the following:

The Golden Gate Bridge is a popular tourist attraction in San Francisco. ***President Roosevelt opened it.***
The Golden Gate Bridge is a popular tourist attraction in San Francisco. ***It was opened by President Roosevelt.***

The second version is easier to process because it follows the order of "known" to "new."

The passive is much more common in written language than in spoken language.

Verbs with two objects have two possible passive structures:
I ***was given*** *this watch by my parents on my 18th birthday.* (The subject of the sentence is "me/I.")
This watch ***was given*** *to me by my parents on my 18th birthday.* (The subject of the sentence is "the watch.")

UNIT 7: Exercises

1 Write the past participle forms for these verbs which are often used in the passive. What are the spelling rules for each group? Use your dictionary if necessary.

a arrest, invent, jail, murder
arrested, ... Rule: add ed
b accuse, create, produce, prosecute
c classify, identify, try, copy
d acquit, ban, kidnap, mug
e build, grow, make, steal

Rearrange the past participles into two groups according to their meaning. Use your dictionary if necessary.

Verbs used to describe crime	Verbs used to describe processes
arrested	*invented*

2 Look at the following notices and announcements. Use your dictionary if necessary. Underline the passive structures and name the tenses.

a The movie was written, directed, and produced by Steven Spielberg. *Simple past*
b Passengers are requested to remain in their seats until the plane has come to a complete standstill and the engines have been turned off.
c Lunch is now being served.
d Feeding the penguins is strictly prohibited.
e Applications must be submitted by December 31.
f The management cannot be held responsible for any loss of property.
g Pills to be taken three times daily.

Where would you expect to see these notices or hear these announcements? Discuss with a partner.

3 Write affirmative and negative passive sentences. Use the verb in parentheses and an appropriate tense.

a My mother (be born) ________________ in the 1950s.
My mother was born in the 1950s. / My mother wasn't born in the 1950s.
b She (bring up) ________________ in a small village.
c She (educate) ________________ at a private school.
d She (teach) ________________ English from the age of eleven.
e She (award) ________________ a scholarship to study at college.
f She (marry) ________________ in the local church.
g She (employ) ________________ by the same company for the last twenty years.

Check (✓) the sentences which are true for you. Write three (true) passive sentences about your mother (or someone else in your family).

4 Look at these general knowledge facts. Cross out *by* + the agent if it is not necessary.

a Chess was invented in India by Indians.
b Snakes are not found in Ireland by anybody.
c 20% of the body's energy is used by the brain.
d The Statue of Liberty was built in France by French people.
e Fourteen muscles are used by people to smile.
f Forty-three muscles are used by people to frown.
g The first disposable safety razor was patented by King Camp Gillette.

How many of the facts did you know?

5 Rewrite these sentences in the passive. Start each sentence with *I*.

a People gave me money for my last birthday. *I was given money for my last birthday.*
b My friend is showing me around her new apartment this evening.
c My employers don't pay me very much.
d People have sent me over twenty text messages so far today.
e Teachers taught me how to swim before I was seven.
f People tell me that I look like my father.

Are any of the sentences true for you?

UNIT 8: Modals of deduction. Past perfect

Part 1: Modals of deduction

There are many ways of expressing how certain or uncertain you are about something.

Degree of certainty	Modal auxiliaries	Other phrases
99% certain it IS ✓	It must be ...	I'm sure it's ...
↓	It may be ... It could be ... It might be ...	Perhaps it's ... Maybe it's ...
↓	It can't be ...	I'm sure it isn't ...
99% certain it ISN'T ✗		

*They **must** be home by now. They set off over an hour ago.*
*I **might** arrive late. I have to finish this report first.*
*Who's at the door? It **can't** be Jill – she's on vacation in Florida.*

The opposite of *must be* is *can't be*.
*The keys **can't be** in my coat because I wasn't wearing it. They **must be** in my purse.*

Part 2: Past perfect

Affirmative	Negative	Question	Short answer *Yes*	Short answer *No*
I/You/He, etc. **'d (had) worked.**	I/You/He, etc. **hadn't (had not) worked.**	**Had** I/you/he, etc. **worked**?	Yes, I/you/he, etc. **had.**	No, I/you/he, etc. **hadn't.**

You use the past perfect when you are talking about the past and you want to refer to an earlier past time. The past perfect clearly shows that one past event happened earlier than other past events.

*When we **arrived**, the concert **had already started**.*

*When we **arrived**, the concert **had already started**.*

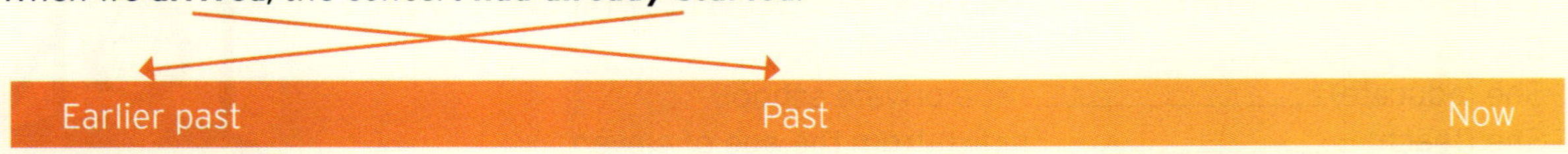

Conjunctions such as *after*, *because*, *by the time*, and *when* are often used to combine a simple past clause with a past perfect one.

*The movie started. I arrived. ➔ The movie had started **when** I arrived.*
*The train left. He reached the platform. ➔ **By the time** he reached the platform, the train had left.*
*He didn't check his tires. He had a flat tire. ➔ He had a flat tire on the highway **because** he hadn't checked his tires.*
*We had lunch. We went for a walk. We took the bus home. ➔ We had lunch and then took the bus home **after** we had been for a walk.*

UNIT 8: Exercises

Part 1

1 Match the sentences so that they make sense.

a I'm going to set up my computer myself. — 3
b You've been driving all day.
c Oh, no. I must be getting old.
d A new car? On my salary?!
e You must be Sarah's husband.
f Congratulations on your engagement.

1 She's told me so much about you.
2 You can't be serious! It's impossible.
3 I'm sure it can't be that difficult!
4 You must be delighted.
5 I'm afraid I can't remember your name!
6 You must be absolutely exhausted.

2 Rewrite these observations with the modal verb in parentheses so that the meaning is the same.

a I'm sure you're really cold! (must)
You must be really cold!
b I'm sure you're kidding. (must)
c I'm sure your keys aren't far away. (can't)
d Maybe you won't enjoy the movie. (might not)
e I'm sure you know who she is. (must)
f I'm sure it's not far from here. (can't)
g Maybe you'll meet the love of your life. (might)
h I'm sure she isn't that old. (can't)

Think about situations when you have made observations like these. Tell a partner.

Part 2

1 Test your irregular verbs. Use the verbs in the box to complete the three lists in the table with the infinitive, simple past, and past participle forms. There are eight verbs in each list.

~~bet~~ burst cost ~~dig~~ ~~drink~~ feed fight fly hurt let mean ring
rise shine shrink shut sing sink slide split spread stick swim win

1 All forms the same	2 Two forms the same	3 All forms different
bet – bet – bet	*dig – dug – dug*	*drink – drank – drunk*

Check your answers on page 167. Underline any verbs you weren't sure about.

2 Work with a partner. In each case write a second sentence, changing the verb in bold into the past perfect.

a I **had** breakfast when I got to work this morning.
I'd had breakfast when I got to work this morning.
b I **read** Harry Potter when I saw the movie.
c I **traveled** a lot when I started my job.
d I **did** the shopping when I got home yesterday evening.
e I **passed** my driving test when I went to college.
f The class **started** when I arrived.

In what way does the use of the past perfect change the meaning of the sentences? Are any of the sentences true for you?

3 Complete the sentences to make them true for you.

a By the time I was [age?], I had learned how to ... (swim? ski? drive? etc.)
b By the age of [age?], I had been to more than [number?] ... (countries? schools? concerts? etc.)
c By the time I was sixteen, I'd been learning [subject?] for [number?] years.
d By the age of [age?], I had moved [number?] times.
e By the age of [age?], I had realized that ...
f By the time I was [age?], I had decided that ...

Compare your sentences with your partner.

UNIT 9: Reported statements and questions

Reporting speech means using your own words to report what somebody has said (or thought).

Direct speech		Reported speech
Ana said, "I don't believe you."	→	Ana **said she didn't believe me.**
I said, "We can talk about it tomorrow."	→	I **told her we could talk about it the next day.**
She said, "Who do you think you are?"	→	She **asked me who I thought I was.**

When you report statements "using your own words", you need to decide which tenses, which pronouns, which time expressions, and which reporting verbs to use. When you report questions, you also need to change the word order.

Tenses

There is usually a logical "back-shift" of tense. This is because what the person said is now in the past. Present becomes past; present perfect or simple past become past perfect; *can* becomes *could*, etc.

Direct speech		Reported speech
"I**'m** really tired."	→	She said she **was** really tired.
"I**'ve had** a great day."	→	He said he**'d had** a great day.
"I **cut** my finger."	→	She said she**'d cut** her finger.
"I**'m going to take** a shower."	→	He said he **was going to take** a shower.
"I **was trying** to open a can of beans."	→	She said she **had been trying** to open a can of beans.
"I **can't find** the time to cook."	→	He said he **couldn't find** the time to cook.
"I **don't want** to go out."	→	She said she **didn't want** to go out.
"I**'ll order** Chinese take-out."	→	He said he **would order** Chinese take-out.

Pronouns

Pronouns (*I*, *she*, *we*, etc.) and possessive adjectives (*my*, *your*, *his*, etc.) may change, depending on who is reporting and who/what they are reporting.

Direct speech: "**I** understand **your** ideas but **I** don't agree with **them**."
Report 1: *My mother told **me** that **she** understood **my** ideas but that **she** didn't agree with them.*
Report 2: *Ted's mother told **him** that **she** understood **his** ideas but that **she** didn't agree with them.*

Expressions of time or place

"Here-and-now" expressions in direct speech may change to "there-and-then" expressions in reported speech.
"Can you **come here tomorrow**?" → *He asked if I could **go there the next/following day**.*

Reporting verbs

The most common reporting verbs are *say* (*that*) and *tell somebody* (*that*). Other verbs such as *admit*, *claim*, *explain*, *insist*, *reply*, or *suggest* can also be used. If you're not sure, use your dictionary to check on the correct verb pattern.
She said it was her fault. (NOT ~~*She said me it was her fault.*~~)
She told me she hadn't been thinking. (NOT ~~*She told that she hadn't been thinking.*~~)
She explained that she had been very tired. (NOT ~~*She explained me that she had been very tired.*~~)

Reported questions

In reported questions, the word order changes to subject + verb. You don't use *do/does/did*.
For *yes/no* questions you use *if* or *whether*.
"How **are you**?" → *He asked me how **I was**.*
"Have you been here long?" → *He asked me **if/whether** I had been there long.*
"Where are you from?" → *He asked me where I **was from**.*

Imperatives

You can report an imperative with *tell somebody to do something* or *ask somebody to do something*.
"Don't worry!" → *She told him not to worry.*
"Hurry up!" → *He asked them to hurry up.*

UNIT 9: Exercises

1 Match the beginnings and the ends of these famously "wrong" predictions and opinions.

a In 1898, the Munich Technical Institute said that
b In 1899, the Commissioner of US Patents said that
c In 1907, Lord Haldane, British Minister of War, said
d In 1927, Harry Warner of Warner Brothers asked
e In 1943, Thomas Watson, IBM chairman, said
f In 1962, the producers of *Doctor No* said that

1 Sean Connery couldn't play the sophisticated James Bond because he looked like a bricklayer.
2 who the heck wanted to hear actors talk.
3 Albert Einstein showed no promise.
4 there was a world market for maybe five computers.
5 everything that could be invented had been invented.
6 the airplane would never fly.

Rewrite the predictions and opinions as quotes.

a *"Albert Einstein shows no promise."*

2 Read the newspaper article about a great-grandmother's lucky escape. Complete the article by changing the direct speech into reported speech.

Lucky escape

A great-grandmother told the newspaper how she escaped death by centimeters after being hit by a meteorite traveling at 480 km/hr. Margaret Smithers said (**1** "It just missed my head and hit my arm.") *it had just missed her head and (had) hit her arm*.

Seventy-six-year-old Margaret was hanging out the laundry in her backyard when the brown metallic stone hit her. She said (**2** "I felt a nasty pain on my arm which started bleeding heavily.") ______________ . Her husband found the five-centimeter rock on the grass. She added that (**3** "I'm glad it didn't hit me on the head") ______________! Experts are analyzing the walnut-sized rock.

A spokesperson from the Astronomical Society said, (**4** "There's a good chance it is a meteorite.") ______________ . But he added that (**5** "The chances of being hit by one are incredibly small.") ______________ . He explained that (**6** "Most meteorites disintegrate as they enter the atmosphere.") ______________ . However, on average, one falls to Earth every week.

3 Complete the sentences with *asked*, *said*, or *told*.

a She ___*said*___ she didn't believe me.
b I ______________ her it was true.
c She ______________ me why I hadn't told her.
d I ______________ I'd wanted to.
e She ______________ she'd been really upset.
f I ______________ her I was sorry.
g She ______________ me if I'd go with her.
h I ______________ her I couldn't.

What do you think the conversation was about? Discuss with a partner.

4 Report the direct speech using the verb in parentheses.

a "I hate spending money on new clothes." (said)
He/She said that he hated spending money on new clothes.
b "I'm not wearing this jacket again!" (told)
c "Do you think I look fat in these pants?" (ask)
d "I need to go on a diet." (said)
e "I've checked the oil and put some air in the tires." (told)
f "Don't forget that it's our anniversary tomorrow." (asked)
g "I don't want to get married until I'm forty." (said)
h "What time does your salsa class finish?" (asked)

Compare your ideas with a partner.

UNIT 10: Defining relative clauses. Real conditionals

Part 1: Defining relative clauses

A relative clause can define the thing or person introduced in the main clause. It comes immediately after the person or thing it is describing. You use *that* (or *who*) for people and *that* (or *which*) for things.

The man ***that/who cuts my hair*** *is named Jo.*
A frog is an animal ***that/which lives on land and in water****.*

The relative pronoun (*that*, *which*, *who*) can be the subject of the verb in the relative clause.

subject verb
People ***who come from*** *Rio de Janeiro are called Cariocas.*

subject verb
A florist is a store ***that sells*** *flowers.*

When the relative pronoun is the subject of the verb, it can never be omitted.

The relative pronoun (*that*, *which*, *who*) can be the object of the verb in the relative clause.

object verb
The work ***that*** *you* ***do*** *is very interesting.*

object verb
The man ***who I met*** *yesterday is a famous artist.*

When the relative pronoun is the object of the verb, it can be omitted.
The work ~~that~~ you do is very interesting.
The man ~~who~~ I met yesterday is a famous artist.

Part 2: Real conditionals

Real conditional sentences – sometimes called "first conditional" sentences – consist of an *if*-clause and a main clause. They are used to talk about present or future situations that are real or possible. These include promises, warnings, and threats.

If the weather improves, we'll go for a walk.
If you quit smoking, I'll be very happy.
If you touch that, you'll burn your finger.
If you don't go now, we'll call the police.

if-clause
In most real conditional sentences, you use a present tense (simple, progressive, or perfect) in the *if*-clause, even when you are talking about the future.

	***if*-clause**	**Main clause**
Simple present	If you **arrive** early,	wait for me in the station café.
Present progressive	If you**'re spending** any time in Rio,	I can recommend a great hotel.
Present perfect	If you **haven't finished** by ten,	you'll miss the mail.
going to	If you**'re going to** talk to me like that,	I'm leaving!
Modal auxiliary	If you **can't** do it,	ask Tom for help.

Unless means the same as *if ... not*.
Unless *you agree ...* = ***If*** *you* ***don't*** *agree ...*

***if*-clause**	**Main clause**
Unless you start studying now / **If** you **don't** start studying now,	you'll never pass your exams.

Main clause
You usually use the simple present, modal auxiliaries (especially *will/won't*, *can*, *must*, and *may*), or the imperative in the main clause.

***if*-clause**	**Main clause**
If he finds out the truth,	it's all over for you and me.
	we'll be in big trouble.
	you can forget about our vacation in Cuba.
	deny everything!

The *if*-clause and the main clause can often go in either order.
If I feel like going out, I'll give you a call. OR *I'll give you a call if I feel like going out.*
Use a comma after the *if*-clause when the *if*-clause comes before the main clause.

UNIT 10: Exercises

Part 1

1 Make one-sentence definitions using the relative pronouns *who/which/that*.

- **a** A rolling pin is a kitchen utensil. You use it to flatten pastry.
  A rolling pin is a kitchen utensil which/that you use to flatten pastry.
- **b** A pestle is a tool. You use it to crush nuts and seeds.
- **c** A woodlouse is a small insect. It eats dead wood.
- **d** A farrier is a person. He/She makes and fits horseshoes.
- **e** A fandango is a dance. It originated in Spain.
- **f** A burglar is a person. He/She breaks into your house and steals things.

Check (✓) the sentences in which the relative pronoun can be omitted.

2 Insert a relative pronoun *who/which/that* where necessary.

- **a** The school I went to was near my house.
- **b** My mom is the only person really understands me.
- **c** The issue worries me most is global warming.
- **d** The biggest party I've had was for my 21st birthday.
- **e** I've got a lot of friends live in Ecuador.
- **f** I think it's better to have a job you enjoy than to have a well-paid job you hate.
- **g** The people live next door to me are really friendly.

Which sentences are true for you? Discuss with a partner.

Part 2

1 Match the two halves of the sentences.

a	They're not going skiing tomorrow	**1**	if you leave now.
b	I'm not going to go for a walk	**2**	unless they get fresh snow.
c	You'll miss your flight	**3**	if they want me to.
d	You can still get your train	**4**	unless you help me with my French.
e	I won't help you with your German	**5**	if it's raining.
f	I'll take care of their children	**6**	unless he studies hard.
g	He won't pass his exams	**7**	if she really concentrates.
h	She'll be top of her class	**8**	unless you take a taxi to the airport.

2 Look at the advice given by children to children and underline an appropriate alternative.

- **a** **Unless** / **If** you get a bad grade at school, don't show it to your mom, **unless** / **if** she's on the phone.
- **b** Don't make an enemy of the school bully **unless** / **if** he's smaller than you.
- **c** **Unless** / **If** your mom is angry with your dad, don't let her brush your hair.
- **d** **Unless** / **If** you like being hit, don't tell your mom her diet's not working.
- **e** Don't hit your sister **unless** / **if** your parents are out.
- **f** **Unless** / **If** your dad asks, "Do I look stupid?", don't answer him.
- **g** **Unless** / **If** you want a kitten, start off by asking for a horse.

Which do you think is the best/funniest piece of advice? Discuss with your partner.

3 Write real conditional sentences using the verbs in brackets.

- **a** If the weather (be) ____*is*____ good next weekend, I (go) ____*'ll go*____ for a long run.
- **b** If it (rain) ________ tomorrow, I (not go) ________ out.
- **c** My friends and I (go) ________ to the beach tomorrow if it (be) ________ sunny.
- **d** If I (earn) ________ enough money this year, I (visit) ________ the USA.
- **e** I (go) ________ snowboarding this winter, if there (be) ________ enough snow.
- **f** I think I (see) ________ my family this weekend, unless I (have to) ________ work.

Which sentences are true for you?

UNIT 11: Wishes and regrets. Unreal conditionals

Part 1: Wishes and regrets

I wish / If only are two ways of talking about unreal situations. You can use them to express wishes or regrets about the present or the past. After *I wish / If only*, the tense backshifts to show that the situation described is/was unreal (see below).

Tense changes		
Fact		**Wish/Regret**
I'**m** a teacher.		If only / I wish I **wasn't/weren't** a teacher.
Simple present	➔	Simple past
I'**m going** to the concert with Adam.		I wish / If only I **was going** with Carl.
Present progressive	➔	Past progressive
I **haven't studied** any other languages.		I wish / If only I **had studied** another language.
Present perfect	➔	Past perfect
I **left** school early.		If only / I wish I **hadn't left** school early.
Simple past	➔	Past perfect

Other (non-tense) changes	
Fact	**Wish/Regret**
I don't have **enough/much** time.	If only / I wish I had **more** time.
I'm not very **good at** math.	If only / I wish I was/were **better at** math.

Part 2: Unreal conditionals

Unreal conditional sentences consist of an *if*-clause and a main clause. When forming unreal conditional sentences, the tense backshifts in the *if*-clause to show that the situation described is/was imaginary.

if-clause

To show that a present (or future) situation is imaginary, you use a past tense.
To show that a past situation is imaginary, you use the past perfect.

Fact		Imaginary situation
I'**m not** a teenager.	➔	If I **was/were** a teenager, ...
I **didn't tell** him.	➔	If I **had told him**, ...

If I/he/she/it were is more formal than *If I/he/she/it was*.
You always use *were* in the fixed expression *If I were you* ...

Main clause

For a present or future situation, you usually use *would/wouldn't* + infinitive in the main clause.
For a past situation, you usually use *would/wouldn't* + *have* + the past participle in the main clause.

if-clause	Main clause
If I **could** sing,	I'**d be** in a band.
If I'**d had** a map,	I **wouldn't have gotten** lost.

Note: Unreal conditional sentences which refer to imaginary situations *in the present* (or future) are sometimes called "second conditional" sentences. Unreal conditional sentences which refer to imaginary situations *in the past* are sometimes called "third conditional" sentences

UNIT 11: Exercises

Part 1

1 Make sentences, using *I wish* or *If only*.

a I can't play the piano.
I wish I could play the piano.
b I don't live near a beach.
c I don't like my job.
d I'm getting old.
e I don't have enough free time.
f I'm not good at English.
g I have such a stressful life.
h I don't earn a lot of money.

Which are true for you?

2 Complete the second sentence so that it means the same as the first.

a I regret I wasn't born in another country.
I wish ... I had been born in another country.
b I regret that I didn't study English more at school.
If only ...
c I regret that I didn't go to a better school.
I wish ...
d I regret that I didn't travel much when I had the chance.
If only ...
e I regret that I got married so young.
I wish ...
f I regret that I didn't work hard in college.
If only ...

Work with your partner. Discuss each regret and say if you share it.

Part 2

1 Write complete questions.

a What / you / do / if / you / find / $100 / in the street?
What would you do if you found $ 100 in the street?
b If / you / be / able to / change your nationality, / what / you / be?
c If / you / can / have dinner with a famous person, / who / you / choose?
d If / you / have to / change one part of your body, / what / it / be?
e What / you / do / if / you / see / someone stealing something in a store?
f If / you / can / meet / one person from history, / who / you / like it to be?

Now answer each question so that it's true for you. Write full answers to each question.

a If I found $ 100 in the street, I'd keep it.

2 Make conditional sentences about these past situations, starting with *If* ...

a I wasn't paying attention. I walked into a lamppost.
If I'd been paying attention, I wouldn't have walked into a lamppost.
b I studied hard. I passed my exams.
c I didn't study hard. I failed my exams.
d I forgot to set my alarm clock. I overslept.
e I missed the bus. I was late for work.
f I bought a lottery ticket. I won some money.
g I didn't have a map. I got lost.
h The weather wasn't good. We didn't go camping.

Have any of these situations happened to you in the last year? Discuss with a partner.

3 Complete these sentences so that they are true for you.

a If I had time, ...
b I'd have been really happy if ...
c If I were very rich, ...
d If I had been born a member of the opposite sex, ...
e If I were president of my country, ...
f I'd have been furious if ...

Work with a partner. Compare your sentences. Are any the same?

UNIT 12: have/get something done

You can use *have something done* (*I'm going to **have my house painted**.*) when someone does something for you – often because you have paid them to do it. As a slightly more informal alternative to *have something done*, you can also use *get something done*.

Form: *have/get* + something (object) + past participle
*I'll probably **get my hair cut** next week.*
*Have you **had your ears pierced**?*
*You really should **get your eyes tested**.*

Compare the two sentences:

- *Mandy cut her hair last week.*
- *Mandy had her hair cut last week.*

In the first sentence, Mandy cut her own hair. In the second sentence, someone else cut her hair and was probably paid for it.

Sometimes *have something done* can mean you have a (usually) negative experience.
We had our house broken into yesterday.
This doesn't mean that you arranged for somebody to break into your house, but that something unfortunate happened to you.
I had my bike stolen last week.
He tried to cheat the Mafia and ended up having his legs broken.

UNIT 12: Exercises

1 Read the sentences and underline the most appropriate verb form in each case.

a We're **redecorating our house** / **having our house redecorated** right now. I'll be glad when the painters have finally finished and left.
b I'm going to **clean my car** / **have my car cleaned** later, so I bought a new pressure washer.
c Do you really think Angelina Jolie is ugly? I think you need to **test your eyes** / **have your eyes tested**.
d We're going to **fix the roof** / **have the roof fixed** soon. We have to wait until the builders can do it.
e I'm **cooking dinner** / **having dinner cooked** for some friends this evening. We get together once a week, and tonight it's my turn to be the host.
f My wife just **repaired her car** / **had her car repaired**. It's great that she's such a practical person – and it saves us a lot of money!

2 Complete the sentences with *have/get* + *something* + past participle, using the verb in parentheses.

a We (deliver) ________________ take-out ________________ to our home every week.
b I always (service) ________________ my car ________________ at the same garage.
c I (cut) ________________ my hair ________________ once a month.
d I usually (check) ________________ my teeth ________________ every six months. I've got a really good dentist.
e We (do) ________________ odd jobs ________________ in our house by professionals.
f I (take) ________________ my passport pictures ________________ in a professional studio. They look much better.

Work with a partner. Discuss which sentences are true for you.

3 Using the prompts, make questions with *have/get* + *something* + past participle.

a You / ever / appearance / change
Have you ever had your appearance changed?
b How often / you / eyes / test
c You / ever / anything / steal
d You / ever / ears / pierce
e You / ever / your car / vandalize
f How often / you / hair / cut

Work with a partner. Take turns asking and answering the questions.

Test yourself!

Underline the correct option in each sentence.

Units 7-9

21 I can't stand (a) **wait** (b) **to wait** (c) **waiting** around.

22 He asked me (a) **help** (b) **to help** (c) **help** him.

23 She promised (a) **come** (b) **coming** (c) **to come** at 10:00 a.m.

24 Our office is (a) **cleaning** (b) **being cleaned** (c) **cleaned** right now.

25 The nominations (a) **have** (b) **has** (c) **having** been announced.

26 The lights aren't on: Sam must (a) **be** (b) **was** (c) **have been** out.

27 We (a) **are** (b) **have been** (c) **were** too late: the train had already left.

28 I knew I (a) **haven't** (b) **hasn't** (c) **hadn't** been there before.

29 She said that she (a) **'ll** (b) **'d** (c) **'ve** bought some new clothes.

30 We asked him (a) **whether** (b) **when** (c) **how** he had ever had problems.

Score: ____ /10

Units 10-12

31 A truant is a pupil (a) **who** (b) **he** (c) **which** stays away from school without permission.

32 If you (a) **wanted** (b) **will want** (c) **want** to join us, bring some food.

33 Jon won't come (a) **unless** (b) **if** (c) **if not** you ask him.

34 They wouldn't be so popular if they (a) **weren't** (b) **wouldn't be** (c) **aren't** so talented.

35 Do you know how she (a) **does feel** (b) **feels** (c) **feel**?

36 If I (a) **can** (b) **could** (c) **would** sing, I'd be in a band.

37 I wish I (a) **took** (b) **have taken** (c) **had taken** swimming lessons when I was at school.

38 If I (a) **'ve** (b) **'d** (c) **'d have** had a map, I wouldn't have gotten lost.

39 She's wearing (a) **an expensive white silk** (b) **a white expensive silk** (c) **a silk white expensive** blouse.

40 I'm having my eyes (a) **test** (b) **tests** (c) **tested** tomorrow.

Score: ____ /10

Glossary

main verb | adjective | conjunction | modal auxiliary verb | adverb | article | pronoun | main verb

Learn these useful words and you can understand more about the language you are studying.

determiner | noun | pronoun | main verb | preposition | noun | auxiliary verb

Agents are people or things that perform an action in a passive sentence.
He was brought up by ***his aunt and uncle.***

Antonyms are words that mean the opposite of other words.
rich ✣ *poor* *dead* ✣ *alive* *tall* ✣ *short*

Back-shift is when a verb moves "one tense back" in a conditional clause or reported statement.

If you ***were*** *a woman, you'd understand.*
"I can't come." → *He said he* ***couldn't*** *come.*

Clauses are groups of words containing a subject and a verb.

main clause	subordinate clause	main clause
I waited	*but she didn't come.*	*I'll call*

time (subordinate) clause
when I get there.

Note: Subordinate clauses are introduced by conjunctions.

Collocation refers to words that frequently occur together.
common sense *get along well* *Merry Christmas*

Complements refer to adjective or noun phrases which give more information about the subject of a clause.
She was ***very happy***. *It's* ***my fault***. *I feel like* ***a complete idiot.***
Note: Complements usually follow verbs like *be, seem, feel.*

Conjunctions show a connection between one clause and another.
Just as *we were leaving the hotel, I spotted a friend.*

Consonants are all the letters of the English alphabet except for the five vowels *a, e, i, o,* and *u.*
b, c, d, f, g, h, j, k, l, m, n, p, q, r, s, t, v, w, x, y, z

Expressions are groups of words that belong together where the words and word order never or rarely change.
black and white *That reminds me.* *How do you do?*

Idioms are groups of words with a meaning which cannot be understood by taking the meaning of each individual word.
My father ***footed the bill.*** *Let's* ***play it by ear****, OK?*

Intransitive verbs do not take an object.
He ***arrived.*** ***Is*** *Marta still* ***sleeping****?* *Stop* ***shouting!***
Note: Many verbs can be either intransitive or transitive. It depends on the meaning or context.
He ***opened*** *the door.* (Transitive)
The door ***opened.*** (Intransitive)

Linkers show a connection between one sentence and another.
Many drivers drive too fast. ***As a result****, there are more and more accidents.*

Numbers can be cardinal (*1, 2, 3, ...*) or ordinal (*1st, 2nd, 3rd, ...*).

Objects usually come after the verb and show who or what is affected by the verb.
She closed ***the door.*** *My dog hates* ***me.***
I made ***a cup of coffee.***

Note: Some verbs take both a direct object (DO) and an indirect object (IO).
She gave ***him*** (IO) ***a kiss*** (DO). *He sent* ***her*** (IO) ***some flowers*** (DO).
I teach ***students*** (IO) ***English*** (DO).

Participles are the forms of verbs used in compound tenses and as adjectives.
What are you ***doing****?* *I've* ***finished.*** *It's* ***freezing!***
He's ***injured.***

Particles are the adverbs or prepositions that form part of a phrasal verb.
turn it ***on*** *take* ***off*** *get* ***along with*** *her*

Partitives are words or expressions that show that only part of something is being referred to, rather than all of it.
a piece of *cake* ***a pack of*** *gum* ***a bunch of*** *flowers*

The **phonetic alphabet** is a set of special symbols which shows speech sounds in writing.
mother = /ˈmʌðər/ coffee = /ˈkɑfi/

Phrasal verbs are combinations of a verb and one or two particles.
switch on *come up with*

Pronouns are words used in place of nouns or noun phrases. There are many classes of pronoun.
Subject pronouns: *I, you, she*, etc.
Object pronouns: *me, you, her*, etc.
Possessive pronouns: *mine, yours, hers*, etc.
Demonstrative pronouns: *this, that, these, those*

Proper nouns are words that refer to a particular person, place, or institution.
Janet, Mexico City, the United Nations

Proverbs or sayings are short, well-known statements that give practical advice about life.
When the cat's away, the mice will play.

Register describes a level and style of a piece of language which is appropriate for the circumstances in which it is used.
I am very grateful for your help. (More formal) *Thanks.* (More informal)

Relative clauses are clauses that modify a noun or a noun phrase. They give additional information about the noun and are joined to a previous clause by words such as *who, that,* or *which.*
That's the man ***who helped me.*** *This the pen* ***(that) I lost.***
Everyone is well, ***which is really great.***

Synonyms are words or expressions which mean the same as another word or expression.
tolerate sb = put up with sb *I'm off now. = I'm going now.*

Transitive verbs take an object.
You're wasting ***your money.*** *He cut* ***his finger.***
I can't pronounce ***"comfortable."***

Vowels are the letters *a, e, i, o,* and *u.*

Audioscript

Unit 7

2.02

(H = Host; J = Jack)

H: People are increasingly obsessed with reading stories and looking at pictures of celebrities. Today there are more paparazzi on the streets than ever, all of them trying to get the definitive celebrity picture. We're here with Jack, a paparazzo with fifteen years of experience, about his job. Jack, thank you for joining us.
J: You're welcome.
H: Jack, why are people so interested in reading about the private lives of celebrities?
J: Because they're young, beautiful, rich, and photogenic, and they lead glamorous lifestyles.
H: But the pictures that appear in the tabloid press are not always glamorous. They're often unflattering pictures of celebrities just trying to lead their lives. For example, I remember seeing a picture of Matt Damon getting a parking ticket. What's so interesting about that?
J: Well, people also want to think that these celebrities are just normal people, so they enjoy seeing pictures of them doing ordinary things like shopping. I also think it's fine to take unflattering pictures of them because it gives us hope when we realize that they're just like us really!
H: I understand that, but where do you draw the line?
J: Well, we're not completely insensitive. We try not to involve children. For example, Kate Moss asked us not to take pictures of her daughter, and we haven't. Do you remember seeing pictures of her daughter in the press?
H: No, but I did read an interview with Kate Moss, where she said that she can't walk anywhere because the paparazzi follow her everywhere. That must be awful. In the same interview she said that a female photographer was chasing her in New York and fell over a water hydrant. She cut her lip and was bleeding, so Kate stopped to ask her if she was OK. The woman just continued taking pictures! That's a little desperate, isn't it?
J: The woman was just doing her job. Listen, so many of these celebrities refuse to cooperate with the paparazzi. We try reasoning with them. We explain that we don't want to upset them, but they shout and swear at us. So we follow them everywhere. It's a game. Have you ever seen a bad picture of Nicole Kidman in the press?
H: Er, no.
J: That's because she plays the game. She always agrees to smile for the camera, and we get our shot. Then we leave her alone. If you ask me, I think these celebrities are hypocritical. On the one hand they need to have their pictures in the press, and on the other hand they tell us that we're invading their privacy. If they don't like the attention, I suggest that they change jobs.

2.04

/t/ checked, escaped, forced, stopped
/d/ described, involved, named, used
/Id/ expected, needed, reported, treated

2.05

a Talks between the UN and delegates from major African nations have been suspended after the African team stormed out, complaining about budget issues. After three weeks of non-stop discussions, the chief negotiator has called for a one-week cooling-off period before talks start again.
b President Liga has announced his resignation after a difficult 12 months in office. He will remain until the end of the year and then step down, allowing Vice President Lopez to take his place.
c Hundreds of holidaymakers slept on beaches last night as forest fires continued to sweep through the Mediterranean. Foreign consulates are working hard to help many travelers who want to return home.
d Skywatchers in the US are preparing for the spectacular sight of a total solar eclipse. The moon is set to pass in front of the sun, casting a shadow that will sweep over the nation from Oregon in the west to South Carolina in the east. It is the first total solar eclipse to be seen exclusively in the US since independence in 1776. The next is not due until 2024.
e High school student Elana Banker has been barred from returning to school after the summer vacation. The reason: the tattoos that she acquired during the vacation, which are banned according to the school rules. The Principal, Brad Martin, says Elana will not be allowed to return until she has had the tattoos removed.
f A jogger caught on camera pushing a woman into the path of an oncoming bus in London England, has been arrested thanks to a huge response from the public. The police put out a request for help after failing to find the man for two months. One of the man's co-workers came forward when they saw the TV appeal.

2.07

Positive responses
Good job!
Lucky you!
Oh, congratulations!
Oh, that sounds interesting.
How exciting!
Negative responses
Oh, I'm sorry to hear that.
Oh, no, that's terrible.
How annoying!

2.08

a We got engaged last week.
b My internet's down again.
c I'm going snowboarding for the first time this weekend.
d I just won $1,000 in the lottery.
e I'm reading Barack Obama's autobiography.
f My wallet was stolen.
g My mom's going to give me her car.
h I think my boyfriend might lose his job.
i I passed all my English exams.

Unit 8

2.09

(W = Woman; M = Man)

W: Have you heard from Conrad lately? Is he still going around the world?
M: Yes, lucky guy. He's in South America now - I had a message from him yesterday.
W: How's he doing?
M: He's having a great time. Come and take a look at the pictures on his blog.
W: Oh, great.
M: Here we go.
W: Oh, wow! Look at those waterfalls. Where is that?
M: Well, he hasn't put the name of the place, but I guess it could be Vietnam.
W: Or it could be India.
M: No, it can't be India, because he hasn't been there. I'm pretty sure it's Vietnam. I know he went trekking in the hills there.
W: Oh, I'd love to go to Vietnam.
M: Mm, me, too. Now this one must be Singapore. Look at that skyline - it's so built-up.
W: Or it could be Hong Kong.
M: No, he didn't go to Hong Kong, but I know he stopped off in Singapore.
W: Ah. Wow, look at these statues. They look really old. Is it a Buddhist temple?
M: Yes, I think so. That's probably Thailand. He was there for the New Year.
W: Lucky guy. Now this is different. I didn't know Conrad could ride a horse.
M: He can't. I don't think that's him.
W: So where is this then?
M: I'm not sure, but it's probably southern Argentina.
W: Oh look, here's a good one. What is he doing?!

2.11

Continents
Asia, Antarctica, Europe
Mountain Ranges
the Himalayas, the Andes, the Pyrenees
Oceans
the Pacific, the Atlantic, the Indian
Rivers
the Nile, the Amazon, the Danube

2.12

[P = Peter; M = Marc]

P: Hi Marc, how's it going?
M: All good thanks. Have you recovered from your jet lag?
P: Just about - I slept till noon today.
M: So, when can I take you to dinner? I'm free this Friday if you are?
P: Ah, sorry no. My parents have invited me for dinner on Friday. How about Saturday?
M: Err ... I had planned to ... see someone on Saturday...
P: Oh yes? Did you meet someone while I was away?!
M: Err ... well, this is what I wanted to talk to you about over dinner ... it's Carla.
P: ... Marc ... you are joking aren't you? Please tell me you are joking ...

2.13

I once went on a trip through the Sinai desert in Egypt, from the Red Sea to a historical place called St. Catherine's Monastery. I was actually on a windsurfing vacation with some friends in a small resort called Dahab. It's a perfect place for windsurfing and other water sports. But one day, the weather was terrible for windsurfing; basically, there was no wind at all. My friends decided to go diving, but I don't like being under the water, and I hate lying on the beach. So I signed up for a trip to St. Catherine's Monastery. We left the hotel at about 10:00 a.m., and the weather was just beginning to get hot. There were ten of us in a minivan including eight tourists, one guide, and one driver. Fortunately, the minivan had air-conditioning. The guide spoke five languages, so during the trip, he told us the history of the monastery in English, Spanish, French, and German. The trip took about two hours, and as we drove through one of the driest deserts in the world, I just stared out of the window at the wonderful scenery. The sandy color of the mountains looked fantastic against the blue sky. We stopped once on the way at a place where the view is spectacular and everybody got out and took pictures. There were Bedouins selling souvenirs, and I bought a beautiful necklace. By the time we arrived at the monastery, it was really hot and there were a lot of other tourists there, but I was glad I'd come. It's a very special place, and I'd love to do the trip again, but next time I'd rent a car and do it on my own time.

2.16

Tim called his girlfriend, Fiona, at Los Angeles International airport last Monday. He was at the gate and about to board his plane to the UK. He was visiting for the second time and they talked about their plans for the weekend. That was the very last time Fiona heard from him. He didn't arrive at Fiona's apartment in West London and he has not been seen since.

Fiona called the police who did some investigating together with the Californian authorities. Northeast Airlines employees remember seeing Tim at the gate, and their records show that Tim checked in and took the flight. But there is no record of him entering the UK. Several passengers interviewed by police were certain that seat 32B - which was Tim's seat - was empty for the whole flight. His phone was switched off and he didn't return to his Santa Monica home. So, it's a complete mystery! What has happened to Tim?

Unit 9

2.17

No one wants to appear superficial when using social media. Nowadays it seems most people want to make a statement when they post on the internet. Many people turn to different online environments where they can tell their friends their opinions on a great variety of issues, such as politics, food, travel, shopping, entertainment, news, etcetera. See below for current trends in internet use.
On politics: 63% of people *said* that they liked to express how they voted on social media whereas 30% didn't like to risk causing offence to friends so *preferred* to keep their political opinions private. A minority, 7%, thought it was boring to read about other people's political views online.
On food: 27% *stated* that they posted successful recipes online to share with friends, while 13% *admitted* that they had read food blog posts and had watched demo videos but rarely cooked anything themselves. The majority of respondents reported that they had surfed the net for good recipes before having friends round for a meal.
On travel: The majority of people thought that the best way to research destinations and make bookings was via the net (55%) and a lot of people (43%) enjoyed sharing their experiences via blogs. Only 2% *preferred* to keep quiet about their travel in case their favorite places were over-run with tourists.
On shopping: The vast majority of respondents (65%) *said* that they had bought their clothes online.
24% *explained* that they had looked at their favorite brands on the net, then went to the mall to try them on before they made a purchase. Only 11% *claimed* that they had bought mostly from stores.
On entertainment: 68% *said* that they had downloaded or streamed most of their videos and movies from the net.
25% *preferred* to use the net mainly to catch up on TV programs. A minority of 7% *declared* that they rarely used the internet for entertainment.
On news: 59% *insisted* that they had the news from social media rather than from the newscasts or newspapers. 38% *said* that they looked at Twitter first when a news item broke and only 3% said that they had *refused* to use social media for news.

2.18

1
A: Which is your favorite track on the album?
B: The last one - it's amazing. I can't wait to see them performing live.
2
A: What did you think of it?
B: I thought the acting was fantastic and the cinematography's superb. Apart from that, it was so boring.
3
A: Have you finished it yet?
B: Almost.
A: What's it like?
B: Really good. I think it's going to be a bestseller.
4
A: I enjoyed that. What did you think of it?
B: I thought it was awful - a sentimental tearjerker - and the ending was predictable.
A: Well, it made you cry anyway.
B: No, it didn't - I've got a cold.
5
A: Are you enjoying it?
B: Yes. It was a little difficult to get into, but now that I'm past the first few chapters, I can't put it down.
6
A: What did you think of the special effects?
B: What special effects?
A: It was all done with computers.
B: Oh, no. I thought it was real. You've spoiled it now.
7
A: Did you have a good time?
B: Not really. I can't stand all that techno stuff. I like it when you can actually hear the lyrics.
A: Old hippy.
B: What did you say?
A: Nothing.

2.20

One of my favorite movies is *Forrest Gump*. I know it's an old movie but I've never seen anything better. Actually, I've seen it three times. The last time I saw it was the other night on TV, and it made me laugh and cry all over again. I love Tom Hanks and I think he's great in this movie. Robin Wright played the part of his girlfriend, and Sally Field was his mom. I can't remember who else was in it, or who directed it. But I do know that it won six Oscars including best picture, best director, and Tom Hanks got best leading actor.
Apparently it's based on a novel, but I have no idea who wrote it. There are so many things I love about this movie. I guess it's a drama, but it's historical and it's funny and it's really sad, too. The character of Forrest Gump is amazing. He's not very smart, and at the beginning of the movie he can't walk properly, but he manages to succeed in life without meaning to, and without realizing it. I particularly like the parts where he meets famous people like President Kennedy or Elvis Presley. It's so good the way they mix old black and white footage from the 60s. It's hilarious when Forrest meets Elvis. Forrest has a strange way of walking, and when Elvis imitates him, it looks like the dance that he was famous for.
The soundtrack is great too. There are all these classic rock songs including some by Elvis. But the ending is a tearjerker - I cry my eyes out every time. I won't spoil it for you in case you haven't seen it, but you should see it because it's the best movie of all time.

2.25

M: Hey, Rosa! I need the car tonight. I'm going to that gig downtown and I said I would give Mike and Jeff a ride. That's OK, right?
W: Not going to happen, Rob. I need the car in case Mom needs picking up from the station - she's arriving this evening, remember?

2.26

M: Hey, Rosa! I need the car tonight. I'm going to that gig downtown and I said I would give Mike and Jeff a ride. That's OK, right?
W: Not going to happen, Rob. I need the car in case Mom needs picking up from the station - she's arriving this evening, remember?
M: Oh, come on. I've promised. How about doing a favor for your favorite brother?
W: Sorry, I told Mom that I'd pick her up if she needed it. You'll have to get a taxi.
M: I don't have the money. Look - if I can have the car tonight, you can have it for the rest of the weekend.
W: You're just not listening, Rob. It's my car and it's a no.
M: But what do I tell Mike and Jeff...?
W: Sorry, not my problem. Look at the time - you'd better get going. The bus leaves in 5 minutes...

REVIEW C

2.28

Bryn: Hi there, you're listening to WBC on 94.6 FM and I'm your host, Bryn Partridge. This morning we are talking about Prince Harry's recent outburst at the media. What do you think about this? Do you agree that the media are too intrusive or do you think it's important we know what the British royal family is up to? Give me a call, I am ready and waiting to hear your views. We have our first caller ... Megan from West Virginia. Hi Megan, what do you think about all this?
Megan: Hi, Bryn. I just wanted to say I completely agree with Prince Harry.
Bryn: You do?
Megan: Yes, I think it is outrageous that the British royal family have no privacy at all. They are human beings just like us and none of us would like to be watched all the time!
Bryn: Thank you, Megan. I think we have Charlie on the line?
Charlie: Hi, Bryn. I think it's a bit of a fuss about nothing. What do they expect? Everyone wants to know about them - why shouldn't they put up with a bit of intrusion?
Bryn: Ah, so you think it's part of their job do you, Charlie?

Charlie: I do. They have to be popular. They represent their people. If they have to smile and pose for the camera whenever they go out, what's the problem?

Bryn: Thank you, Charlie. I think we're going to hear from Steven now. Hello Steven, are you there?

Steven: Yes, I am, Bryn. I'm British and I totally disagree with your last caller. If we want our royal family to represent us around the world we have to respect them and give them some space. If they are constantly stressed how are they going to do their job properly? Ordinary people have no idea how hard it must be to live your life under a microscope and have every move watched and judged...

Bryn: Well, thank you, Steven, you have put your view across very clearly. It's time to go to the news now, but we'll be back with more of your calls in a couple of minutes...

Unit 10

2.29

1

A: It's something that lived a very long time ago. It looks very scary.

B: A thing that lived a long time ago.

C: Um ... It's a big monster.

2

A: It's a person who takes care of animals when they are sick.

B: A person that helps animals.

C: It's the doctor that takes care of our pets.

3

A: It's something that's very cold and it's ...it's a ... it's a stone.

B: It's kind of a big piece of ice that cracks off a bigger piece.

C: It's a big ice cube.

4

A: A place where animals have been put up to show people.

B: Somewhere where they show you things that are very old.

C: It's somewhere people show things like dinosaurs and olden days things.

5

A: It's a person who takes toys away.

B: It's someone that comes in the middle of the night ... and he has ... something on his face with round holes and he has a T-shirt that's black and white and he robs things.

C: It's someone who steals things when you're asleep.

2.31

Dale: Welcome to Dale's Dilemmas. I'm Dale Rogers, and the subject of today's dilemma is pushy parents. Are today's parents too ambitious for their children? Should they let children be children and stop organizing their lives? Should we congratulate them for developing their children's potential, or should we say "back off and leave the kids alone"? In the studio, we have George and Rachel from Chicago. They disagree about how to bring up their daughter, and we're going to hear what they have to say. ... George and Rachel, welcome to the show.

M: Thanks.

W: Thanks.

Dale: Rachel, if we could start with you. Can you tell us a little about your daughter?

W: Yes, my daughter Hayley is five years old, and I think she has what it takes to be a movie star. So I'm doing everything I can to get her into the movies.

Dale: And what exactly does that involve?

W: Hayley goes to acting classes twice a week. She has a singing teacher who comes to the house once a week, and we watch a lot of movies together at home. Then on weekends we go to auditions. Sometimes we have to travel to New York or Los Angeles, but I'm willing to do whatever it takes.

Dale: That's a lot of traveling. What do you think about it, George?

M: I think my wife is obsessed. I don't think she should make Hayley do this. It isn't Hayley's choice. Rachel wanted to be a child star, and that's why she's making Hayley go though this.

W: I'm not making her do anything against her will. Hayley loves it and she wants to be a star.

Dale: But at five years old, does she understand what it means?

W: No, of course not. I want to let Hayley grow up like a normal child. There's too much pressure in the movie world. She's a kid. Let her play, let her have friends.

Dale: It's true that being a child star can be a very isolating experience.

W: I know that, but if you don't try, you don't succeed. When Hayley is famous and she's making movies, you're going to look back and thank me.

Dale: Thank you, Rachel and George. In just a moment, we'll be meeting Mark and Charlene, who want their two-year-old son to be the next Tiger Woods. But first, it's over to the studio audience. Who has a question for Rachel and George?

2.32

Dale: Who has a question for Rachel and George? Yes, the woman in the red dress, please ...

W2: Do you know how Hayley feels?

W: She enjoys her life and she wants to be a movie star.

M: I think she's too young to know how she feels. She says she's happy because she wants to please her mom.

Dale: Thank you. Another question now, please. Yes, the woman with the blue shirt.

W3: Can you tell me what you're going to do when Hayley starts school?

M: I'd like her to stop doing auditions and focus on being a normal school kid.

W: Well, I think it would be wrong to stop now after all the time and money we've invested. After all, you don't invest in a business and then give up after six months if you're not making a profit.

M: But Hayley is not a business - she's a child. Our daughter.

Dale: OK, ... let's have one from the man in the green jacket.

M2: Do you think you're depriving Hayley of a normal childhood?

M: Yeah. I worry about that.

W: Well, I don't. She's special and I want to help her to fulfill her potential.

Dale: Yes, the young man with the gray sweater.

M3: Could you tell me whether you have any other children and how they are affected?

M: We have a seven-year- old son, and he misses his mom.

W: He's very proud of his little sister.

Dale: The woman in the red dress again.

W2: Do you have any idea how stressful it is to be a movie star?

M: Very stressful. I don't think my wife has thought about the negatives at all.

W: We can cope. I just hope that I can come back here in ten years and we can do a follow-up story when Hayley's a star.

Dale: Well, I'm afraid that's all we have time for now. Thank you to our guests...

2.34

My mother plays the piano really well, so she wanted me to learn the piano, too. I had lessons for a while, but I wasn't very good, and eventually my piano teacher begged my parents to stop sending me. So that was the end of my music career! But what I really wanted to do was martial arts, and my parents let me join a club when I was about nine. I used to love those kung fu movies and Bruce Lee was my hero. I had posters of him all over my room, and that was how I got the idea. I was a little disappointed at first, because our classes weren't like the movies, but then I got obsessed with it and I was doing martial arts two or three times a week. We did it at a gym on the other side of town, so my parents drove me there because it was pretty far away from my house. But when I was about fourteen, I decided that I didn't want my friends to see my parents dropping me off, so I took the bus instead. I'm still doing martial arts now after ten years, and I've started getting more and more interested in kick-boxing. I'd definitely encourage my own children to do martial arts. It's not just about fighting - of course, you learn self defense - but you also learn other skills such as mental discipline and self-confidence.

2.37

a

I took my three year-old, Johnny, with me to the grocery store yesterday. It was a disastrous outing and it ended with him crying loudly because I wouldn't buy him a bag of candy. I tried to be strong and calm but he just would not listen even when I told him he was a very naughty boy and I was very unhappy. I gave him the candy to make him quiet, but by that time he was so furious he threw them onto the floor. Finally, I had to drag him out of the store crying and shouting. It was so embarrassing. When we got home I made him sit on his own on the bottom step for 5 minutes as a punishment, though I'm not sure he understood why. Maybe I should have given him the candy at the very beginning!

b

Ellie, who normally has a sunny personality, was not in a good mood at all the other day. Maybe she had needed a snack before we left for the supermarket, but anyway, by the time we got there she was in a very bad mood. She started complaining and pulling things out of the cart that I had put in. I kept calm and told her that was making me feel angry. But I could see things were getting worse, so I gave her a comic from the shelf and an apple from the cart, and sat her in the cart to look at the comic. As soon as she started looking at it and took the first bite of the apple, I praised her for behaving well. I asked her about the apple - what it tasted like, what color it was, to distract her. She read the comic and ate her apple all the way round the store. The checkout girl even commented on how good she was, which was lovely. In the car going home I told Ellie she made me feel very proud when she sat so quietly in the cart.

Unit 11

2.41

M1: Why don't you tell me something that I would never have guessed?

M2: Err, I like to snowboard.

M1: Huh?

M2: That's right, it doesn't even exist! And voice-over acting, you don't know what that is, do you?

M1: Nope but if I did know, I don't think I would want to do it. So, if you didn't become a super star - what did you do?
M2: Hey, listen I didn't do things exactly like you wanted, but I have done some things. Look, I wrote some novels.
M1: Great, I'm very pleased, oops ... did you get any less clumsy?!

2.42

a
I picked up the money and put it in my pocket and went into my office. I thought about it for a long while and then I walked out of the office and went to the local police precinct to hand the money in. I doubt whether the person who dropped the money - about 5,000 dollars in total - would have noticed it had gone, much less have gone to the cops to report it missing, but if I hadn't given it in, I couldn't have lived with myself. The good news is that the cops told me that if it isn't claimed in six months, I can keep the cash!

b
I decided to keep quiet. I figured that it was none of my business. My friend's boyfriend may just have been carried away by the circumstances. I do want to be honest with my best friend but I don't want to be the reason they split up.

c
Ed went back to the restaurant the next day and paid the difference. The restaurant owner was so grateful; he gave us some vouchers for a free main course when we next go to the restaurant.

2.44

Conversation A
1 Hello.
2 Is Maddy there?
3 Is this Phil?
4 Hold on, I'll go and get her.
5 It's me.
6 What are you up to later?
7 See you tomorrow.

Conversation B
1 Good morning.
2 I'd like to speak to Mr. Moore, please.
3 Who's calling, please?
4 Just a moment, please. I'll try to put you through.
5 Philip Jones here.
6 Are you available later on today?
7 I'll look forward to seeing you tomorrow.

2.45

Brainstorming
How is it that some people always seem to be able to generate new ideas and think creatively, and others seem to struggle to do so?
Well, the good news is that you can learn to think creatively using brainstorming techniques. Nobel prize winner Linus Pauling said: 'The best way to have a good idea is to have lots of ideas'. A brainstorming session is a great way to generate a whole bunch of ideas - and it's fun. The rules are simple:
- everyone in the group has a say
- all ideas are accepted
- no criticism of others' ideas is allowed

Unit 12

2.46

1 Al
I'm really proud of my fabulous Mexican snakeskin cowboy boots. Most of my friends hate them and wouldn't be seen dead in boots like these, but I like that fact that they're different. I wear them for work with a suit and tie, and I think the contrast looks great. I like to stand out from the crowd.

2 Fran
I usually wear jeans and a sweatshirt during the day, but for going out, my favorite thing is my red low-waisted miniskirt. I wear it with a wide black leather belt and short boots, and it looks fantastic with my old black leather jacket.

3 Jay
I have about twenty-five pairs of jeans, but my favorites are my old black skinny jeans. I play the guitar in a band and I always wear my black skinny jeans and a black turtle neck sweater when we're playing. It's like a uniform.

4 Brooke
I'm really into vintage clothes and I just bought a beautiful long purple silk evening dress. I haven't worn it yet - I'm waiting for the right occasion. It would look great on the red carpet at the Oscars.

2.47

a /i/ medium green jeans
b /u/ two blue suits
c /ɜr/ third worse fur
d /ɔ/ tall bald author
e /eɪ/ plain beige suede
f /er/ wear their hair

2.48

I was invited to a friend's birthday party recently, and there were a few people there who I'd never met before. I'm not very good at introducing myself to strangers, so I just stayed with the people I knew, and that was great because I hadn't seen them for a while. But then this woman came over and introduced herself, and asked who I was. I thought she seemed really friendly and very confident. She was tiny, with long curly black hair, and I remember she was wearing a beautiful turquoise necklace. I admired the necklace, and she told me that it was from Mexico. We talked about Mexico, and it turned out that we'd both been on vacation to the same Mexican resort, but not at the same time. Small world. I haven't seen her since then, but she works with my friend, so I think I'll probably run into her again some time. I hope so.

2.49

A: Did you see Ten Years Younger last night?
B: No, I missed it. I had to work. Why, was it good?
A: It was amazing. They had a man and a woman on, and honestly, the transformation was incredible.
B: What did they look like?
A: Well, the man looked about sixty, even though he was forty-nine.
B: Oh, no!
A: He had this long gray hair, and he was dressed a little like an old rock star.
B: Urgh!
A: Anyway, he had his hair cut and colored, and he had his teeth whitened.
B: Oh yes, that makes such a difference.
A: And I think he had his eyelids lifted.
B: Oh well, of course, if you can afford to have plastic surgery, you're bound to look better.
A: Yes, but I think that's all he had done. Oh, and he had his clothes chosen by a stylist.
B: What about the woman? Did she have lots of plastic surgery?
A: No, she didn't actually. But she looked as if she'd had a major face-lift. It was amazing. Before the makeover, everybody thought she was about forty-nine, but she was thirty-seven.
B: Oh. What did she have done?
A: She had her hair cut and colored, of course. And she had her make-up done by an expert and her clothes chosen by a stylist.
B: Oh, I'd love that. How old did they think she was after the makeover?
A: Thirty-two.
B: Oh, she must have been thrilled. Hey, do you think I need to have my hair cut?

2.52

Making positive comments
a Oh, she looks so beautiful.
b What a beautiful day!
c This dessert is delicious.

Giving and receiving compliments
d What a beautiful dress!
Oh, this? I've had it for ages.
e Blue really looks good on you. Do you think so? Thank you.
f That's a very nice hat.
I'm glad you like it.

Thanking and accepting thanks
g Thank you so much for a wonderful day.
You're welcome.
h Thank you for inviting us.
Don't mention it.

REVIEW D

2.54

I: Colin, tell me about your childhood. You never knew your real parents, did you?
C: That's right. I was brought up in children's homes. I moved several times when I was very young and then went to live with my foster parents, Ida and Bud, when I was ten.
I: Was it a difficult childhood?
C: Well, some people might see it that way, but I have very good memories. In that part of New York at that time, everyone was poor – we never had any money – but we didn't complain. There was a real neighborhood spirit. Everyone helped each other.
I: Can you tell me what your memories of that time are?
C: We used to make our own entertainment - there was no TV, no video games. We played in the streets and down by the railroad tracks. All the kids together.
I: And you left school pretty young, didn't you?
C: Yes. I left school at fourteen and went to work in a factory. But I didn't like it. I only stayed there two years. I always wanted to work for myself, so I became a cab driver. I worked as a driver for ten years until after I got married.
I: But you didn't stay a cab driver?
C: No. I was ambitious! I wanted a good life for my kids. So when we had our third baby, I started my own business from nothing. Soon had fifty taxi cabs and drivers! I sold the business a few years ago, and made enough money to buy a second home in Florida.
I: How did you meet your wife?
C: We met at a dance. She was wearing a beautiful yellow silk dress. I thought she was the prettiest thing I'd ever seen. We got married six months later.
I: Any regrets? Would you change anything about your life?
C: Not a thing! I feel like the luckiest man in the world!

Phonetic symbols

Vowels

/ɪ/	ship	/ʃɪp/	(build, business, gym, spinach, women)
/i/	need	/nid/	(bean, he, key, niece, people, sardine)
/ʊ/	put	/pʊt/	(could, foot, woman)
/u/	pool	/pul/	(flew, fruit, lose, rule, shoe, through, two)
/e/	egg	/eg/	(breakfast, friend, many, said)
/ə/	about	/əˈbaʊt/	(arrive, husband, lemon, nervous, police)
/ɔ/	saw	/sɔ/	(abroad, caught, talk, thought, water)
/æ/	back	/bæk/	(bag, fast, laugh)
/ʌ/	bus	/bʌs/	(blood, does, enough, onion)
/ɑ/	father	/ˈfɑðər/	(car, heart, pasta)

Diphthongs

/ɜr/	verb	/vɜrb/	(learn, curly, skirt, word)
/eɪ/	face	/feɪs/	(break, eight, fail, say, they)
/ɔɪ/	boy	/bɔɪ/	(noise)
/oʊ/	nose	/noʊz/	(although, coat, know, shoulder)
/aɪ/	white	/waɪt/	(buy, die, eye, height, high, my)
/aʊ/	mouth	/maʊθ/	(town)
/ɪr/	hear	/hɪr/	(near)

Consonants

/p/	pen	/pen/	(happy)
/b/	bag	/bæg/	(rabbit)
/t/	tea	/ti/	(ate, fatter, worked)
/d/	dog	/dɔg/	(address, played)
/ʧ/	chip	/ʧɪp/	(natural, watch)
/ʤ/	jazz	/ʤæz/	(age, bridge, generous)
/k/	cake	/keɪk/	(chemistry, kitchen, knock, toothache)
/g/	girl	/gɜrl/	(foggy)
/f/	fat	/fæt/	(different, laugh, photographer)
/v/	very	/ˈveri/	(of)
/θ/	thin	/θɪn/	(think)
/ð/	these	/ðiz/	(they)
/s/	snake	/sneɪk/	(city, message, race)
/z/	zoo	/zu/	(has)
/ʃ/	sugar	/ˈʃʊgər/	(description, machine)
/ʒ/	measure	/ˈmeʒər/	(garage, usual)
/m/	map	/mæp/	(summer)
/n/	name	/neɪm/	(sunny, knife)
/ŋ/	ring	/rɪŋ/	(thanks, tongue)
/h/	house	/haʊs/	(who)
/l/	leg	/leg/	(hill, possible)
/r/	road	/roʊd/	(carry, write)
/w/	wine	/waɪn/	(one, why)
/j/	yes	/jes/	(used, usual)

Stress

Word stress is shown by underlining the stressed syllable: *water, amazing, Japanese*.

Letters of the alphabet

/eɪ/	/i/	/e/	/aɪ/	/oʊ/	/u/	/ɑ/
Aa	Bb	Ff	Ii	Oo	Qq	Rr
Hh	Cc	Ll	Yy		Uu	
Jj	Dd	Mm			Ww	
Kk	Ee	Nn				
	Gg	Ss				
	Pp	Xx				
	Tt					
	Vv					
	Zz					

Irregular verbs

Infinitive	Simple past	Past participle	Infinitive	Simple past	Past participle
be	was/were	been	let	let	let
beat	beat	beaten	lie	lay	lain
become	became	become	light	lit/lighted	lit/lighted
begin	began	begun	lose	lost	lost
bend	bent	bent	make	made	made
bet	bet	bet	mean	meant /ment/	meant /ment/
bite	bit	bitten	meet	met	met
blow	blew	blown	pay	paid	paid
break	broke	broken	put	put	put
bring	brought /brɔt/	brought /brɔt/	read	read /red/	read /red/
build /bɪld/	built /bɪlt/	built /bɪlt/	ride	rode	ridden
burn	burned	burned/burnt	ring	rang	rung
burst	burst	burst	rise	rose	risen
buy /baɪ/	bought /bɔt/	bought /bɔt/	run	ran	run
can	could /kʊd/	(been able)	say	said /sed/	said /sed/
catch	caught /kɔt/	caught /kɔt/	see	saw /sɔ/	seen
choose	chose	chosen	sell	sold	sold
come	came	come	send	sent	sent
cost	cost	cost	set	set	set
cut	cut	cut	shake	shook	shaken
deal /dil/	dealt /delt/	dealt /delt/	shine	shone	shone
dig	dug	dug	shoot	shot	shot
do	did	done	show	showed	shown
draw	drew	drawn	shrink	shrank	shrunk
dream	dreamed/dreamt	dreamed/dreamt	shut	shut	shut
drink	drank	drunk	sing	sang	sung
drive	drove	driven	sink	sank	sunk
eat	ate	eaten	sit	sat	sat
fall	fell	fallen	sleep	slept	slept
feed	fed	fed	slide	slid	slid
feel	felt	felt	speak	spoke	spoken
fight	fought /fɔt/	fought /fɔt/	spend	spent	spent
find	found	found	split	split	split
fly	flew	flown	spread	spread	spread
forget	forgot	forgotten	stand	stood	stood
forgive	forgave	forgiven	steal	stole	stolen
freeze	froze	frozen	stick	stuck	stuck
get	got	gotten	swear	swore	sworn
give	gave	given	swell	swelled	swollen/swelled
go	went	gone/been	swim	swam	swum
grow	grew	grown	take	took /tʊk/	taken
hang	hung	hung	teach	taught /tɔt/	taught /tɔt/
have	had	had	tear	tore	torn
hear	heard /hɜrd/	heard /hɜrd/	tell	told	told
hide	hid	hidden	think	thought /θɔt/	thought /θɔt/
hit	hit	hit	throw	threw	thrown
hold	held	held	understand	understood	understood
hurt /hɜrt/	hurt /hɜrt/	hurt /hɜrt/	wake	woke	woken
keep	kept	kept	wear	wore /wɔr/	worn
kneel	knelt/kneeled	knelt/kneeled	win	won /wʌn/	won /wʌn/
know	knew /nju/	known	write	wrote	written
lay	laid	laid			
lead	led	led			
leave	left	left			
lend	lent	lent			